Bayard Taylor Hainer

Hainer's manual of the Oklahoma school land laws

Bayard Taylor Hainer

Hainer's manual of the Oklahoma school land laws

ISBN/EAN: 9783337145446

Printed in Europe, USA, Canada, Australia, Japan

Cover: Foto ©Suzi / pixelio.de

More available books at **www.hansebooks.com**

HAINER'S MANUAL

OF THE

Oklahoma School Land Laws

Rules and Regulations Governing the Leasing of

SCHOOL LANDS

CHEROKEE STRIP AND KICKAPOO BILLS.

Suggestions to Homesteaders.

BY

BAYARD T. HAINER.

Attorney=at=Law,

GUTHRIE, OKLAHOMA.

GUTHRIE, OK.
STATE CAPITAL PRINTING CO.
1893.

TABLE OF CONTENTS.

HAINER'S MANUAL,

1893.

ORGANIC ACT.

Section 18 of the Organic Act of Oklahoma Territory provides that sections numbered sixteen and thirty-six in each township in said Territory shall be. and the same are hereby reserved for the purpose of being applied to public schools in the state or states hereafter to be erected out of the same.

ACT OF MARCH 3, 1891.

Section 36 of the Act of Congress of March 3. 1891, entitled, "An act making appropriations for the current and contingent expenses of the Indian Department, and fulfilling treaty stipulations with the various Indian tribes, for the year ending June thirtieth, eighteen hundred and ninety-two, and for other purposes," provided that the school land reserved in the Territory of Oklahoma by this and former acts of Congress may be leased for a period not exceeding three years for the benefit of the school fund of said Territory by the Governor thereof, under regulations to be prescribed by the Secretary of the Interior.

RULES AND REGULATIONS.

The general rules and regulations so far prescribed by the Secretary of the Interior are as follows:

1. The Governor shall execute the leases, for such periods as he may deem best, in the several cases, not exceeding three years in any case.

2. The quantity of school land in Oklahoma to be leased to any one person, under the thirty-sixth section of the act of March 3, 1891, shall not exceed one quarter section, *except* in the country comprised of Beaver, "D," "E," "F," "G" and "H" counties, and the Cherokee Outlet, west of range thirteen of the Indian Meridian, when the same shall have been opened to settlement, in which country the maximum quantity allowed to be leased shall be one section, or 640 acres.

3. Sealed bids shall be received by the Governor at his office, after proper public notice, to be given in the manner deemed by the Governor the best practicable under the circumstances, and the lease to be awarded to the actual bidder at the highest amount of rent bid in each case.

4. The period of payments of rent shall be fixed in the leases by the Governor at his discretion, according to the circumstances of each case, with security satisfactory to him to be required for the payment thereof when due, should he deem it necessary, and forfeiture to be provided for each in case of failure.

5. The leases after they have been executed by the Governor, shall be forwarded to the Secretary of the Interior for his approval.

6. After the leases are approved by the Secretary of the Interior and returned to the Governor, they shall be recorded by the Secretary of the Territory according to section 3 of the Organic Act of Oklahoma.

7. In case a new lease is to be made at the expiration of the lease, the preference shall be given the former lessee, if the Governor finds that he cultivated the land in a business-like manner, and fulfilled the terms of the lease in good faith.

8. The money, after deduction of the necessary expenses incurred in the leasing, must be treated as a part of the territorial school fund, and be placed to the credit of said fund in the custody of the territorial treasurer, to be appropriated as the legislature of the Territory may enact.

9. All necessary expenses of purchasing records, stationery, office rent and for clerk hire and advertising, shall be paid out of the fund obtained from the leasing, and must be approved by the Secretary of the Interior.

10. The Governor shall make a report to the Secretary of the Interior at the end of each calendar year, or as soon as practicable thereafter.

11. The precise form and methods of procedure shall be left to the judgment of the Governor subject to the above general rules.

SCHOOL LANDS IN OKLAHOMA PROPER.

That portion of Oklahoma opened to settlement by Act of Congress approved March 2, 1889, is known as and commonly called Oklahoma proper. This country embraces in round numbers 105,200 acres of school land or 670 quarter sections, and is situated in the following counties to-wit: Oklahoma, Cleveland, Payne. Logan, Canadian and Kingfisher. This does not include the school lands attached to these counties by the opening to settlement the lands embraced in the Iowa, Sac and Fox, Pottowatomie and Absentee Shawnee Reservations on the east of Oklahoma, or the Cheyenne and Arapahoe country on the west.

AMOUNT LEASED IN OKLAHOMA PROPER.

By a reference to Governor Seay's annual report for the fiscal year ending June 30, 1892, to the Secretary of the Interior, I find that in Oklahoma proper there are in round numbers 600 quarter sections or 96,000 acres leased and only 70 quarter sections or 11,200 acres unleased.

WHEN AND HOW LEASED.

On April 6, 1891, Governor Geo. W. Steele, commenced the leasing of school lands in Oklahoma Territory, under the Act of Congress approved March 3, 1891. The school lands in Oklahoma proper and Beaver county were advertised for leasing for three consecutive weeks in the leading newspapers of each county. Sealed bids were received by the Governor and the leases were awarded to the highest actual bidder in each case. The leases were made to run for a period of three years from April 6, 1891. Hence *these leases* will expire on April 6, 1894, and all lessees who desire to re-*lease* the *land*, under this first public leasing, must make their application in writing to the Governor on or before January 1, 1894, as specified in the lease. The lands leased under this first advertisement embrace the greater portion of the best school lands in Oklahoma proper.

The minimum yearly rental fixed by Governor Steele, at this leasing was $16.00 per quarter section, except in Beaver connty where the minimum yearly rental was placed at $8.00 per quarter section. The rental was fixed by the Governor to be due and payable on the first day of January of each year. The lessees were required to give notes with approved personal security for each annual payment *except* where the lessee paid first year's rental in advance; in such cases no security was required for the two deferred payments. These lease notes do *not* bear interest until after due, when they draw interest at the rate of 7 per cent. per annum until paid.

JULY 18TH, 1891, LEASING.

The second public leasing in Oklahoma prop er was on July 18, 1891. This leasing embraced all school lands not leased under the April 6, 1891, leasing. These leases expire on July 18, 1894, and all applications to re-lease must be made on or before April 1, 1894, in order to receive the benefit of a preference right.

PRIVATE LEASING.

Bids will be received at any time by the Governor for any vacant and unleased school lands that have been heretofore advertised and still remain unleased upon like terms and conditions as at the public leasings. This is called "private leasing."

SCHOOL LANDS ADVERTISED FOR LEASING MARCH 4, 1892.

The school lands embraced in that portion of Oklahoma which was formerly the Sac and Fox, Pottowatomie and Absentee Shawnee Reservations were advertised for leasing by proclamation of Governor Seay March 4, 1892. The proclamation provided:

FIRST, That these lands may be leased for a period not exceeding three years from February 1, 1892.

SECOND, That the minimum yearly rental for a quarter section was $25.00.

THIRD, That the leases would be awarded to the highest bidder in each case.

FOURTH, That no preference would be given to persons who settled upon or made improvements on the lands prior to the time of leasing.

FIFTH, That lessees were not allowed to cut or remove any timber.

SIXTH, That no person was permitted to lease more than a quarter section.

In pursuance to this proclamation sealed bids were received by the Governor up to and including April 4, 1892, when the bids were opened and the leases awarded to the highest bidder in each case. By this proclamation 68,960 acres or 431 quarter sections of school land was subject to lease.

Governor Seay's annual report to the Secretary of the Interior shows that at the close of the fiscal year, June 30, 1892, there were 130 quarter sections, or 22,800 acres, of these lands leased. A large portion of the school lands in Pottawatomie county are still unleased. This is no doubt due to the fact that a large portion of the school quarters are heavily covered with timber and as the rules do not permit lessees to cut timber for buildings, fencing or fuel or for clearing purposes, they are of no practicable use for the time being for agricultural purposes and hence are not in demand.

SCHOOL LANDS IN THE CHEYENNE AND ARAPAHOE COUNTRY.

On July 7, 1892, Governor Seay issued his his proclamation to lease the school lands in that part of Oklahoma, which was formerly a part of the Cheyenne and Arapahoe reserves, and embraced in Kingfisher, Canadian, C, D, E, F, G and H counties. The notice provided that these lands would be leased for a period of two and one-half years, from August 1, 1892, and that no person would be permitted to lease more than one quarter section until February 1, 1993. From and after February 1, 1893, any unleased sections or parts of sections in counties D, E, F, G and H may be leased by sections. The yearly rental was fixed at $25.00 per quarter section. The proclamation also contained the usual provision that the lessees would not be allowed to cut or remove or permit to be cut or removed any timber and that no preference would be given to any parties who had settled upon or made improvements on any of said lands prior to the leasing thereof.

In pursuance to this notice nearly all of the best quarter sections in Kingfisher and Canadian counties have been leased. In Blaine county about one-half of the school land is taken, while in counties D, E, F, G and H only a very small per centage so far has been leased.

BEAVER COUNTY.

Governor Seay in his annual report for the year ending June 30, 1892, to the Secretary of the Interior says: "In Beaver county there are in round numbers 1,000 quarter sections of school land, and up to the present time only a small percentage of these lands have been leased. I find from the records that only twenty leases have been granted. This county is mainly adapted to stock raising, and as the rules have heretofore allowed only 160 acres to be leased to one person there was no demand, comparatively speaking, for the leasing of these lands. However, since this rule has been modified recently by the Hon. Secretary of the Interior, so that any person may lease an entire section if he so desires, I confidently believe that hereafter there will be a greater demand for the leasing of these lands, and consequently much larger revenue will be derived for the common school fund.

SCHOOL LANDS IN THE CHEROKEE OUTLET.

The bill providing for the opening of the Cherokee Outlet to settlement by act of congress, approved March 3, 1893, provides that sections 16 and 36 in each congressional township shall be reserved for public school purposes and may be leased in like manner by the Governor of Oklahoma under the regulations prescribed by the Secretary of the Interior, as the school lands were in old Oklahoma and in the Cheyenne and Arapahoe country.

The school lands in the Cherokee Outlet will embrace in round numbers 320,000 acres of land, and by leasing one quarter section to each person there will be in round numbers 2,000 quarter sections to be leased. As the school lands in Oklahoma, by the Organic Act, are reserved for the benefit of the public schools, no person is permitted to settle upon said lands, or make any improvements thereon, without first obtaining a lease therefor, and any person who violates this provision is a trespasser and liable to prosecution as such. And in view of this law, applicable to all school lands in Oklahoma which have been opened to settlement since the Organic Act of Oklahoma went into effect, no person should settle upon or make improvements upon any of these lands until he can do so legally, after a lease has been duly executed to him.

As soon as these lands will be ready for leasing by the Governor of the Territory, they will be advertised in the newspapers in the respective counties where the lands are situated.

These notices will provide as to the time and manner in which bids will be received for the leasing of these lands. The same rules and regulations are applicable to the school lands in the Tonkawa, Pawnee and Kickapoo countries.

PAYMENT OF RENT.

The lessees of school·lands are required to pay the rent annually to the Governor of the Territory ón the 15th day of December of each year. This regulation was made by Governor Seay—making all notes due uniformly on said date.

The notes bear interest at the rate of 12 per cent per annum after they become due and until paid. No interest is charged until the notes fall due.

When the lessee executes his contract for the lease he must also execute his note with approved personal security for the payment of the rental for each year; these notes must be given with personal security to be approved by the Governor of the Territory for the payment of each year's rental. It is imperative that surety be given on all notes in accordance with the instructions of the Secretary of the Interior.

The lessee must also at the time he executes the notes with sureties authorize a confession of judgment by the Attorney General in case of failure to pay the rental, on the back of each note before a Notary Public, or any other officer who can legally administer an oath having a seal.

The lease does not require to be acknowledged by the lesse, but simply signed by him and duly witnessed.

EXPIRATION OF LEASES.

The Secretary of the Interior has vested the power of fixing the time for leases to begin and expire in the Governor of the Territory, provided, that no lease shall exceed a period of three years.

When Governor Steele commenced the leasing of school lands in Oklahoma on the 6th day of April, 1891, in accordance with the act of Congress approved March 3, 1891, and the regulations prescribed by the Secretary of the Interior, he advertised the lands to be leased for a period of three years from the 6th day of April, 1891, thus making the leases expire on the 6th day of April, 1894. The second advertisement for leasing was in July, 1891. All leases executed under this advertisement ran for a period of three years from the 18th of July, 1891. Thus it will be seen that no uniform time was fixed for the expiration of leases.

When Governor Seay assumed the duties of his office he recommended numerous changes to the Secretary of the Interior, which were adopted, relative to the leasing of these lands in Oklahoma, and among these changes were that all leases should expire uniformly on the first day of February. The minimum yearly rental was also changed by Governor Seay from $16 per annum per quarter section to $25 per annum.

TRESPASS ON SCHOOL LANDS.

All occupants or settlers upon school lands except those who have secured leases under section 36, of the act of March 3, 1891, are trespassers. Section 13 of the act of March 2, 1889, provides that: "The lands acquired by the United States under such agreement shall be a part of the public domain to be disposed

of only as herein provided, and sections 16 and
36 of each township, whether surveyed or unsurveyed, are hereby reserved for the use and
benefit of the public schools, to be used within
the limits of said lands under such conditions
as may hereafter be required by Congress."

Section 18 of the Organic Act of Oklahoma
provides that: "Sections numbered 16 and 36
in each township in said Territory shall *be* and
hereby the same *are reserved* for the purpose of
being applied to public schools in the state or
states to be erected out of the same." These
lands, therefore, having been *reserved* by act of
Congress *from settlement*, the Department cannot recognize a settler thereon. Hence, there
can be no such thing as a *bona fide* settler on
school lands in Oklahoma. And it will be observed from the foregoing provisions that no
preference or advantage can be derived by a
person entering upon or improving school land
before a lease is obtained thereto.

MINING.

The lessees of school lands are not allowed
to mine or remove or permit to be mined or removed any minerals from the land leased.

QUARRYING.

The lessees are not permitted to quarry or
remove or permit to be quarried or removed,
any building or other stone, *except such as may
be necessary for the foundations for buildings to
be erected on the leased premises.*

TIMBER.

The laws of the United States prohibit **any**

person from cutting growing timber on school lands in Oklahoma Territory. The fact that a person has leased school land does not grant him the right or privilege to cut or remove or permit to be cut or rem...ed any growing timber from the leased land *for any purpose whatever*, and any person who violates this plain provision of the statute, not only forfeits his lease, but is liable in a civil suit for damages, and to criminal prosecution. The school lands in Oklahoma by the Organic Act are *reserved for the purpose of* being applied to the public schools in the State or States hereafter to be erected out of the same, and the cutting of timber for fencing, building, or domestic use is in direct violation of the provisions of the statute.

The intent and purpose of Congress in making these reservations was to secure and preserve a fund for the education of the youth of the Territory, and hence it is the duty of the general government to turn these lands over to the State when the Territory shall be carved into one, in an enhanced rather than a diminished condition, and that in leasing these lands the lessee has no right to use the estate in any manner whatever, which will tend to deteriorate the value of the lands, when it shall become the duty of the general government to vest the title in the State or States for the use and benefit of the common schools.

FORFEITURE OF LEASES.

The leases provide that upon the non-payment of rental at the time the same shall become due and payable or upon the failure or refusal of the lessee to furnish additional security for any deferred payments, when requested so to do by the Governor, or if the lessee shall fail in any manner to comply with the provisions of the lease or violate any of the conditions thereof, the Governor may at his option declare the lease forfeited and the Governor or any person lawfully entitled to the possession thereof, on behalf of or representing the United States shall have the right to take immediate and peaceable possession of the premises, together with the improvements and growing crops thereon.

IMPROVEMENTS.

In case the lessee is not desirous of releasing the premises, at the expiration of his term of lease, at the highest rental offered by any responsible bidder, should there be competing bids, for the same tract of land, he, the lessee has the right, and is granted the privilege to sell or remove any or all improvements of a movable character, such as the buildings and and fences that he has placed on the leased premises.

However, in case the lessee is in default for non-payment of rental he is not allowed to remove any improvements until all of such rental is paid.

PERMANENT IMPROVEMENTS.

No provision has been made whereby the lessees, in the event that he does not re-lease the premises, can require the person who shall succeed him to pay for the value of improvements which he has placed of a permanent character on the land, such as orchards, breaking and wells. In other words the lessee muse take his chance to realize any benefit from such permanent improvements which he has placed on the leased premises, as the lands will beyond question be turned over to Oklahoma, when the Territory shall be carved into a state, to be disposed of in such manner as the legislature may direct.

SUB-LEASING OR ASSIGNMENT OF LEASE.

The leases provide that the lessees shall not assign or sub-let any portion of the leased premises and such assignment or sub-letting would be void and work a forfeiture of the lease.

TRANSFER OF LEASES.

While the assignment and sub-letting of leases are not allowed under the regulations prescribed by the Secretary of the Interior, the lessee, however, may surrender his lease and request the cancellation thereof by the Governor, subject to the approval of the Secretary of the Interior, upon condition that the rental for the current year is paid and that a new lease is executed to a responsible party designated by him, the lessee, for the unexpired term upon like terms and conditions as the original lease.

RENEWAL OF LEASES.

The leases provide that the lessees who desire to renew their leases must make their application in writing to the Governor of the Territory, at a certain time designated in the lease. The leases executed by Governor Steele during the month of April, 1891, will expire on April

6, 1894, and in all of these leases the lessees must make their application to renew on or before January 1, 1894, in order that he may have the benefit of a preference right. The application should state clearly and concisely the manner in which the land was cultivated during the term of lease, the number of acres in cultiv. t on, the kind, character a id value of the improvements thereon, also the amount of timber upon the land. It is very important that these applications should be made at the proper time and in accordance with the rules and regulation prescribed by the Secretary of the Interior an the Governor of the Territory. A failure to comply with the rules and regulation of the department will cause much trouble and may result in the loss cf the lease and home.

PREFERENCE TO RE-LEASE.

The lessees who have cultivated the land in a business like manner and have complied in good faith with all the conditions of their leases have a preference to re-lease the premises at the highest rental offered by any responsible bidder, at the expiration of the time for which the lease was made. But the right is reserved, by the Governor, to reject any or all bids.

SCHOOL LEASE FUND.

The money realized from the leasing of the school lands becomes a part of the school fund of the Territory. Section 5, Article 12, Chapter 79, Territorial Laws of 1890, provides: "Whenever there accumulates in the hands of the Terrritorial Treasurer the sum of one

thousand dollars belonging to the permanent
school fund of the Territory, it shall be his
duty to call the said board together, and they
shall apportion that money to the various counties of the Territory, in proportion to the
scholastic population of each: thereupon it
shall be the duty of the Territorial Treasurer
to transmit to the treasurers of the various
counties the sum so apportioned to each
county, and the treasurer of the county shall
treat the same as a part of the permanent
school fund of this Territory, to be dealt with
as hereinafter provided.

"It shall be the duty of the auditing office, of
the Territory to notify the County Clerks of
the various counties that the money has been
forwarded to the County Treasurer, and the
amount thereof, and thereupon the auditing
officer of the Territory shall credit the Territorial Treasurer with the money by him so forwarded, and shall charge the same to the
various counties to which it is transferred, and
the various County Clerks shall charge their
respective County Treasurers therewith as permanent school funds."

Section 1, of the same article requires that
the Territorial Superintendent of Public In-
struction, the Territorial Secretary and the
Territorial Treasurer shall constitute a board
of commissioners for the management and investment of the Territorial School, Territorial
Normal School and Territorial University
funds. Such board shall be organized as follows: The Secretary of the Territory shall be

president, and the Superintendent of Public Instructions shall be secretary thereof. In the absence of either of said officers, the Territorial Treasurer shall act as president, or secretary, as the case may be. Such commissioners when acting as such must act personally: no member thereof can be represented in such board by any other person.

LANDS IN LIEU OF SCHOOL LAND GRANTS.

The general law granting school land indemnity provides that: "Other lands of equal acreage are also hereby appropriated and granted, and may be selected by said State or Territory where section 16 and 35 are mineral lands or are included within any Indian, Military or other reservation, or are *otherwise disposed of by the United States.*" See Section 2275 and 2276 U. S. Revised Statutes as amended by the Act of February 28, 1891.

This general provision seems to be applicable to Oklahoma as well as to all States and Territories in general.

The law provides that the indemnity sections should be made "from any unappropriated surveyed public lands, not mineral in character, within the State or Territory where such losses or deficiencies on school sections occur."

There are three general classes of deficiencies in school lands in Oklahoma, to-wit:

"1. Lands allotted to Indians.

' 2. Lands in Beaver County entered by homesteaders who show actual settlement prior to survey.

" 3. Where sections 16 and 36 are fractional

in quantity, or where one or both are wanting by reason of the townships being fractional, or from any natural cause whatever." 14 L. D. 226.

SALE OF SCHOOL LANDS.

The school lands of Oklahoma cannot be sold so long as Oklahoma remains a Territory, having been reserved by act of congress for the use and benefit of the public schools and to be turned over to the state when the Territory shall be carved into one, to be disposed of in such manner as the legislature may direct. What disposition the legislature of the future state of Oklahoma will make of these school lands would be a mere matter of conjecture by me. Oklahoma, I believe, is the only territory in the United States that has had the privilege of leasing its school lands, which privilege has been a great source of revenue and benefit to the public schools of the Territory. All states, I think, so far, have provided that the school lands may be sold under certain statutory limitations after being leased a specified term of years. These states usually provide for the appraisal of the lands and the improvements thereon separately, giving the lessee the privilege of purchasing the lands at the appraised value or to the highest bidder, and should the lessee fail for any cause to purchase the land occupied by him as leasee the party who purchases the land is required to pay the outgoing lessee the appraised value of such improvements. Should Oklahoma follow the footsteps of Kansas, Nebraska and the territories

recently admitted into the Union the probabil-
i.ies are that some law similar to those will be
enacted by the legislature. However, there is
a sentiment at present that these lands *should
be leased perpetually for the benefit of the common school fund.* As stated before, what this feel-
ing may develop into and what future legisla-
tion will be relative to these lands is a mere
matter of conjecture and all lessees who lease
these lands with the hope of making it their
future and permanent home take their chances,
relying upon the confidence and wisdom of the
future lawmakers of the great commonwealth of
Oklahoma to do what is fair and just in the disposal of these lands.

NEEDED CHANGES,

Experience in leasing school lands in Oklahoma has shown that there is urgent need for
additional rules and regulations to be prescribed by the Secretary of the Interior for the
relief and protection of the tenants occupying
these lands in good faith and who have made
valuable and permanent improvements thereon.
Under the present regulations there is no provision made to compensate the present occupants for any improvements upon their lands,
upon failure to renew the lease.

The leases provide that the lessees who desire to renew their leases will be given preference to re-lease at the highest rental offered by
any responsible bidder. Provided, the Governor has a right to reject any and all bids. In
other words, the lessee must, under the present
regulations enter into competition with any out-

sider when he desires to renew his lease. He would have to enter into competition and bid on his own improvements in order to renew his lease and the only alternative he would have would be either to pay the highest rental offered by any responsible bidder or remove his improvements of a movable character from the land.

This, it seems to me, would work a great hardship and injustice to the present occupants and is liable to breed dissension and foster litigation.

Provision should be made to appraise the rental value of the land and the improvements thereon separately. Where there are no competing bids the lands should be re-leased at the appraised rental value, where the lessee has cultivated the land in a business-like manner. Where there are competing bids the lands should be awarded to the highest responsible bidder in each case, and should the outgoing tenant fail to obtain the lease he should be compensated for the appraised value of his improvements before he gives possession to the incoming tenant. This would produce the largest revenue for the school fund and do justice to all parties. Under the present regulations some lands are leased as high as $230 per quarter section and a quarter section adjoining, equally as valuable, or nearly so, is rented for $30 or $40, and as low as $16 to $25.

Some provision should also be made to protect the tenants in their growing crops. For instance, a great number of the leases will expire on April 6, 1894. This is, as everybody is aware, a great wheat growing country: there will be a great deal sown this fall, and there is no provision at present to protect the tenant in these crops should he fail to re-lease the land. This should be reminded. *Edied.*

THE KICKAPOO BILL.

An act to ratify and confirm an agreement with the Kickapoo Indians in Oklahoma Territory, and to make appropriations for carrying the same into effect.

Whereas, David H. Jerome, Alfred M. Wilson and Warren G. Sayre, duly appointed commissioners on the part of the United States, did on the ninth day of September, eighteen hundred and ninety-one, conclude an agreement with Kickapoo Indians in Oklahoma Territory, formerly a part of the Indian Territory, which said agreement is as follows:

"Articles of agreement made and entered into on the Kickapoo Reservation, in the Indian Territory, on the 21st day of June, A. D., 1891, by and between David H. Jerome, Alfred M. Wilson, and Warren G. Sayre, Commissioners on the part of the United States, and the Kickapoo tribe of Indians, in the Indian Territory, and completed at the city of Washington, D. C., on this 9th day of September, A. D., 1891.

ARTICLE I.

"The said Kickapoo tribe of Indians in the Indian Territory hereby cede, convey, transfer and relinquish, forever and absolutely, without any reservation whatever, all their claim, title, and interest of every kind and character in and to the lands embraced in the following described tract of country in the Indian Territory, to-wit:

"Commencing at the southwest corner of the Sac and Fox reservation; thence north along the western boundary of said reservation to the Deep Fork of the Canadian river; thence up said Deep Fork to the point where it intersects the Indian Meridian; thence south along said Indian Meridian to the North Fork of the Canadian River; thence down said river to the place of beginning.

Article II.

"In consideration of the cession recited in the foregoing article, the United States agrees that in said tract of country there shall be allotted to each and every member, native and adopted, of said Kickapoo tribe of Indians in the Indian Territory, 80 acres of land to conform in boundary to the legal surveys of said land. Each and every member of said tribe of Indians over the age of eighteen years shall have the right to select for himself or herself 80 acres of land to be held and owned in severalty; and that the father, or if he be dead, the mother, shall have the right to select a like amount of land, under the same restrictions, for each of his or her children under the age of eighteen years; and that the Commissioner of Indian affairs, or some one appointed by him for the purpose, shall select a like amount of land, under the same restrictions, for each orphan child belonging to said tribe under the age of eighteen years.

"It is hereby further expressly agreed that no person shall have the right to make his or her selection of land in any part of said tract of country that is now used or occupied, or that has, or may hereafter be, set apart for military, agency school, school farm, religious, town site or other public uses, or in sections sixteen (16) thirty-six (36), in each Congressional township; provided, in cases where any member of said tribe of Indians has heretofore made improvements upon and now occupies and uses a part of said sections sixteen (16) and thirty-six (36), such person may make his or her s lection, according to the legal subdivisions, so as to include his or her improvements. It is further agreed that wherever, in said tract of country, any one of said Indians has made improvements, and now uses and occupies the land embracing such improvements, such Indian shall have the undisputed right to make his or her selection, to conform to legal subdivisions, however, so as to include such improvements.

ARTICLE III.

"All allotments hereunder shall be selected within ninety days from the ratification of this agreement by the Congress of the United States, provided the Secretary of the Interior in his discretion may extend the time for making such selections: and should any Indian entitled to allotment hereunder fair or refuse to make his or her selection of land in such time, then the allotting agent in charge of said work of making such allotments shall, within the next thirty (30) days after said time, make allotments to such Indians, which shall have the same force and effect as if the selections had been made by the Indians themselves.

ARTICLE IV.

"When said allotments of land shall have been selected and taken as aforesaid, and approved by the Secretary of the Interior, the titles thereto shall be held in trust for the benefit of the allottees, respectively, for a period of twenty-five (25) years, in the manner and to the extent provided for in the act of Congress entitled "An act to provide for the allotment of land in severalty to Indians on the various reservations, and to extend the protection of the laws of the United States and Territories over the Indians, and for other purposes." Approved February 8, 1887.

"And at the expiration of the said twenty-five (25) years the title thereto shall be conveyed in fee simple to the allottees or their heirs free from all incumbrances, provided the President may at the end of said period extend the time the land shall be so held, in accordance with the provisions of the above-recited act.

ARTICLE V.

"In addition to the allotments above provided for, and the other benefits to be received under the preceeding articles, and as the only further consideration to be paid for the cession and relinquishment of title above-recited, the United States agrees to pay the said Kickapoo Indians, to be distributed among them per

capita, under the direction of the Commissioner
of Indian Affairs, for the improvement of their
said allotments, and for other purposes for their
benefit, the sum of sixty-four thousand and six
hundred and fifty ($64,650) dollars; provided,
that the number of allotments of land provided
for shall not exceed three hundred (300). But
if the number of allotments shall exceed three
hundred (300), then there shall be deducted
from the said sum of sixty-four thousand and
six hundred and fifty ($64,650) dollars, the sum
of fifty ($50) dollars for each allotment in ex-
cess of the three hundred (300); provided,
however, that should the Kickapoos elect to
leave any or all of said money in the Treasury
of the United States, it shall bear interest at
the rate of five per cent per annum after the
ratification by Congress of this contract.

ARTICLE VI.

"It is hereby further agreed that wherever,
in this reservation, any religious society or
other organization is now occupying any portion of said reservation for religious or educational work among the Indians the land so occupied may be allotted and confirmed to such
society or organization, not however to exceed
one hundred and sixty (160) acres of land to
any one society or organization, so long as the
same shall be so occupied and—used, and such
land shall not be subject to homestead entry.

ARTICLE VII.

"This agreement shall have effect whenever
it shall be ratified by the Congress of the
United States.

Be it enacted by the Sena'e and House of Representatives of the United States of America in Congress assembled,

That said agreement be, and the same hereby is, accepted, ratified, and confirmed,

"That for the purpose of carrying into effect the provisions of the foregoing agreement there is hereby appropriated out of any moneys in the Treasury of the United States not otherwise appropriated the sum of sixty-four thousand six hundred and fifty dollars. And after first paying to John T. Hill the sum of five thousand one hundred and seventy-two dollars for services rendered said Kickapoo Indians and in discharge of a written contract made with said Indians and recommended by the Secretary of the Interior, the remainder to be expended for the use of said Indians as stipulated in said contract; Provided that should said Indians elect to leave any portion of said remaining balance in the Treasury, the amount so left shall bear interest at the rate of five per cent per annum." Provided, That none of the money or interest thereon, which is by the terms of said agreement to be paid to said Indians, shall be applied to the payment of any judgment that has been or may hereafter be rendered under the provisions of the Act of Congress approved March third, eighteen hundred and ninety-one, entitled "An act to provide for the adjudication and payment of claims arising from Indian depredations."

SEC. 2. That for the purpose of making the al-

lotments and payments provided for in said agreement, including the preparation of a complete
roll of said Indians, the pay and expenses of a
special agent, if the President thinks it necessary
to appoint one for the purpose, and the necessary
surveys or resurveys, there be, and hereby is,
appropriated, out of any moneys in the Treasury
not otherwise appropriated, the sum of five thous-
and dollars, or so much thereof as may be
necessary.

SEC. 3. That whenever any of the lands, acquired by this agreement shall, by operation of
law or proclamation of the President of the United
States, be open to settlement or entry, they shall
be disposed of (except sections sixteen and thirty-
six in each township thereof) to actual settlers
only, under the provisions of the homestead and
townsite laws (except section twenty-three hundred and one of the Revised Statutes of the United
States, which shall not apply): *Provided, however,*
That each settler on said lands shall, before making a final proof and receiving a certificate of entry, pay to the United States for the land so taken
by him, in addition to the fees provided by law
and within five years from the date of the first
original entry, the sum of one dollar and fifty
cents an acre, one-half of which shall be paid
within two years; but the rights of honorably discharged Union soldiers and sailors, as defined and
described in sections twenty-three hundred and
four and twenty-three hundred and five of the
Revised Statutes of the United States shall not be
abridged, except as to the sum to be paid as afore

said. Until said lands are opened to settlement by proclamation of the President of the United States, no person shall be permitted to enter upon or occupy any of said lands; and any person violating this provision shall never be permitted to make entry of any of said lands or acquire any title thereto: Provided, That any person having attempted to, but for any cause failed to acquire a title in fee under existing law, or who made entry under what is known as the commuted provision of the homestead law, shall be qualified to make homestead entry upon said lands.

Approved March 3. 1893.

THE CHEROKEE OUTLET.

The following is a full text of that portion of the Indian appropriation bill, approved March 3, 1893, which provides for the opening of the Cherokee Outlet to settlers:

SEC. 10.   That the sum of two hundred and ninety-five thousand seven hundred and thirty-six dollars, payable as hereinafter provided, is hereby appropriated out of any money in the treasury not otherwise appropriated, and the Secretary of the Interior is hereby authorized and directed to contract to pay eight million three hundred thousand dollars, or so much thereof as may be necessary in addition, to pay the Cherokee Nation of Indians for all the right, title, interest and claims which the said nation of Indians may have in and to certain lands described and specified in an agreement concluded between David H. Jerome, Alfred M. Wilson and Warren G. Sayre, duly appointed commissioners on the part of the United States, and Elias C. Boudinot, Joseph A. Scales, George Downing, Roach Young, Thomas Smith, William Triplett and Joseph Smallwood, duly appointed commissioners on the part of the Cherokee Nation of Indians in the Indian Territory, on the nineteenth day of December, eighteen hundred and ninety-one, bounded on the west by the one hundredth degree of west longitude; on the north by the state of Kansas, on the east by the ninety-sixth

degree of west longitude; and on the south by
the Creek Nation, the Territory of Oklahoma,
and the Cheyenne and Arapahoe reservation,
created or defined by executive order dated
August tenth, eighteen hundred and sixty-nine;
which said agreement is fully set forth in the
message of the President of the United States,
communicating the same to congress, known as
Executive Document Numbered Fifty-six of the
first session of the Fifty-second Congress, the
lands referred to being commonly known and
called the "Cherokee Outlet," and said agreement is hereby ratified by the congress of the
United States and the acts of congress that have
been or may be passed regulating trade and in-
tercourse with the Indians, and subject, also, to
certain amendments thereto, as follows:

Amend the same by adding to the first paragraph of article two of said agreement the following words: *"And provided further,* That
before any intruder or unauthorized person occupying houses, lands or improvements, which
occupancy commenced before the eleventh day
of August, Anno Domini, eighteen hundred and
eighty-six, shall be removed therefrom, upon
demand of the principal chief or otherwise, the
value of his improvements, as the same shall be
appraised by a board of three appraisers, to be
appointed by the President of the United
States, one of the same upon the recommendation of the principal chief of the Cherokee Nation, for that purpose, shall be paid to him
by the Nation; and upon such payment
such improvements shall become the

property of the Cherokee Nation: *"Provided,* That the amount so paid for said improvements shall not exceed the sum of two hundred and fifty thousand dollars: And *provided further,* That the appraisers in determining the value of such improvements may consider the value of the use and occupation of the land.

Further amend the same by striking out paragraph three of article two of said agreement and changing the numbers of the subsequent paragraphs to correspond.

And the provisions of said agreements so amended shall be fully performed and carried out on the part of the United States: *Provided,* that the money hereby appropriated shall be immediately available and the remaining sum of eight million three hundred thousand dollars or so much thereof as is required to carry out the provisions of said agreement as amended and according to this act, to be payable in five equal annual instalments, commencing on the fourth day or March, eighteen hundred and ninety-five, and ending on the fourth day of March, eighteen hundred and ninety-nine, said deferred payments to bear interest at the rate of four per cent per annum, to be paid annually, and the amount required for the payment of interest as aforesaid is hereby appropriated: *And provided further,* That of the money hereby appropriated a sufficient amount to pay the Delawares and Shawnees their pro rata share in the proceeds of said outlet shall remain in the Treasury of the United States before which their suit are now pending; and a sufficient amount shall also be retained in the Treasury to pay the freedmen who are citizens of the Cherokee Nations or their legal heirs and representatives such sums as may be determined by the courts of the United States to be due them. Nor shall anything herein be held to abridge or deny to said freedmen any rights to which they may be entitled under existing laws or treaties. The acceptance by the Cherokee Nation of Indians of said agreement, as it is hereby proposed to be amended, and as a full and complete relinquishment and extinguishment of all their title, claim, and interest in and to said lands; but such relinquishment and extinguishment shall not inure to the benefit of any railroad company nor vest in any railroad company any right title or interest in or to any of said lands: *Provided*, said railroad shall be relieved from any other payments of compensation to said Cherokee Nation as required by law for running said railrod across said Cherokee outlet.

And said lands, except the portion to be allotted as provided in said agreement, shall, upon the payment of the sum of two hundred and ninety-five thousand seven hundred and thirty-six dollars, herein appropriated, to be immediately paid, become and be taken to be and treated as a part of the public domain. But in any opening of the same to settlement, sections sixteen and thirty-six in each township, whether surveyed or unsurveyed, shall be, and are hereby reserved for the use and benefit of the public schools to be established within the limits of such lands, under such conditions and regulations as may be hereafter enacted by Congress: *Provided,* That if the Legislative Council of the Cherokee Nation shall deem it more advantageous to their people they may issue a loan for the princial and interest of the deferred payments pledging said amounts of interest and principal to secure payment of such debt.

Sections thirteen, fourteen, fifteen, sixteen, twenty-one, twenty-two, twenty-three, twenty-four, twenty-five, twenty-six, twenty—seven, twenty-eight and the east half of sections seventeen, twenty and twenty-nine, all in township numbered twenty-nine north, of range numbered two east of the Indian Merian, the same being lands reserved by Executive order dated July twelth eighteen hundred and eighty-four, for use of and in connection with the Chiloco Indian Industrial School, in the Indian Territory, shall not be subject to public settlement, but shall, until the further action of Congress, continue to be reserved for the purpose for which they were set apart in the said Executive order. And the President of the United States, in any order or proclamation which he shall make for the opening of the lands for settlement, may make such other reservations of lands for public purposes as he may deem wise and desirable.

The President of the United States is hereby authorized, at any time within six months after the approval of this act and the acceptance of the same by the Cherokee Nation as herein provided, by proclamation, to open to settlement any or all of the lands not allotted or reserved, in the manner provided in section thirteen of the act of Congress approved March second, eighteen hundred and eighty-nine, entitled "An act making appropriations for the current and contingent expenses of the Indian Department and for fulfilling treaty stipulations with various Indian tribes, for the year ending June thirtieth, eighteen hundred and ninety, and for the purposes" (Twenty-fifth United States Statutes, page ten hundred and five): and also subject to the provisions of the act of Congress approved May second, eighteen hundred and ninety, entitled "An act to provide a temporary government of the Territory of Oklahoma to enlarge the jurisdiction of the United States court in the Indian Territory, and for other purposes;" also, subject to the second proviso of section seventeen, the whole of section eighteen of the act of March third, eighteen hundred and ninety-one, entitled "An act making appropriations for the current expenses of the Indian Department, and for fulfilling treaty stipulations with various Indian tribes, for the year ending June thirtieth, eighteen hundred and ninety-two, and for other purposes;" except as to so much of said acts and sections as may conflict with the provisions of this act. Each settler on the lands so to be opened to settlement as aforesaid shall, before receiving a patent for his homestead, pay to the United States for the lands so taken by him, in addition to the fees provided by law, the sum of two dollars and fifty cents per acre for any land east of ninety-seven and one-half degrees west longitude the sum of one dollar and a half per acre for any land between ninety-seven and one-half degrees west longitude and ninety-eight and one-half degrees west longitude, and the sum of one dollar per acre for any land west of ninety-eight and one-half degrees west longitude, and shall also pay interest upon the amount so to be paid for said land from the date of entry to the date of final payment therefor at the rate of four per centum per annum.

No person shall be permitted to occupy or enter upon any of the lands herein referred to, except in the manner prescribed by the proclamation of the President opening the same to settlement; and any person otherwise occupying or entering upon any of said lands shall forfeit all right to acquire any of said lands. The Secretary of the Interior shall, under the direction of the President, prescribe rules and regulations, not inconsistent with this act, for the occupation and settlement of said lands, to be incorporated in the proclamation of the President, which shall be issued at least twenty days before the time fixed for the opening of said lands.

The allotments provided for in the fifth section of said agreement shall be made without delay by the persons entitled thereto, and shall be confirmed by the Secretary of the Interior before the date when said lands shall be de-

clared open to settlement; and the allotments
so made shall be published by the Secretary of
the Interior, for the protection of proposed settlers. And a sum equal to one dollar and
forty cents per acre for the lands so allotted
shall be deducted from the full amount of the
deferred payments, hereby appropriated for.
Provided, That D. W. Bushyhead, having made
permanent or valuable improvements prior to
the first day of November, eighteen hundred
and ninety-one, on the lands ceded by the said
agreement, he shall be authorized to select a
quarter section of the lands ceded thereby,
whether reserved or otherwise, prior to the
opening of said lands to public settlement; but
he shall be required to pay for such selection,
at the same rate per acre as other settlers, into
the treasury of the United States in such manner as the Secretary of the Interior shall direct.

The President of the United States may establish, in his discretion, one or more land offices to be located either in the lands to be
opened, or at some convenient place or places
in the adjoining organized Territory of Oklahoma; and to nominate, and by and with the
advice and consent of the senate, to appoint
registers and receivers thereof.

The sum of five thousand dollars, or so much
thereof as may be necessary, the same to be immediately available, is hereby appropriated,
out of any money in the treasury not otherwise
appropriated, to pay for the services of the appraisers to be appointed as aforesaid, at a rate
not exceeding ten dollars a day for the time

actually employed by each appraiser, and their reasonable expenses, and to enable the Commissioner of Indian Affairs, under the direction of the Secretary of the Interior, to effect the removal of intruders required by the first paragraph of article two of said agreement as amended.

TONKAWA INDIAN LANDS.

SEC. 11. That the sum of thirty thousand six hundred dollars, or so much thereof as may be necessary is hereby appropriated, out of any money in the treasury not otherwise appropriated, the same to be immediately available, to pay the Tonkawa tribe of Indians in the Territory of Oklahoma for all their right, title, claim and interest of every kind and character in and to four townships of land, containing ninety thousand seven hundred and ten and eighty-nine one hundredts acres, more or less, c ded, conveyed and relinquished to the United States by article one of an agreement concluded on the twenty-first day of October, eighteen hundred and ninety-one, between David H. Jerome, Alfred M. Wilson and Warren G. Sayre, duly appointed commissioners on the part of the United States, and said Tonkawa tribe of Indians, which agreement is contained in the message of the President communicating the same to congress, and known as Executive Document Numbered Thirteen, first session Fifty-second Congress, to be paid and applied in the manner provided for in said agreement. And such portion of said amount as may be deposited in the treasury of the United

States shall bear interest at the rate of five per centum per annum, which interest shall be applied as provided in said agreement; and said agreement is hereby accepted, ratified and confirmed.

PAWNEE INDIAN LANDS.

SEC. 12. That the sum of eighty thousand dollars, or so much thereof as may be necessary, is hereby appropriated, out of any money in the treasury not otherwise appropriated, the same to be immediately available, to pay the Pawnee tribe of Indians in Oklahoma, formerly a part of the Indian Territory, for all their right, title, claim and interest of every kind and character in and to all that tract of country between the Cimarron and the Arkansas rivers embraced within the limits of seventeen specified townships of land, ceded, conveyed and relinquished to the United States by said Pawnee tribe of Indians, by article one of an agreement concluded on the twenty-third day of November, eighteen hundred and ninety-two, between David H. Jerome, Alfred M. Wilson and Warren G. Sayre, duly appointed commissioners on the part of the United States and said Pawnee tribe of Indians, which agreement is contained in the message of the President communicating the same to congress, and known as Executive Document Number Sixteen, second session Fifty-second Congress, to be paid and applied in the manner provided in article four of said agreement. And the further sum of five thousand dollars, or so much thereof as may be necessary, is hereby appro-

priated, out of any money in the treasury not
otherwise appropriated, the same to be immediately available, to pay the expenses of making the allotments provided for in said agreement, including the pay and expenses of necessary special agents hereby authorized to be appointed by the President for the purpose of
making such allotments, and to pay the expenses of necessary re-surveys therefor. Said
agreement is hereby accepted, ratified and confirmed. And the residue of the proceeds of the
surplus lands mentioned in said agreement
shall be placed to the credit of said tribe in the
treasury of the United States, and shall bear interest at the rate of five per centum per annum,
said interest to be paid and distributed to said
tribe as provided in said article four.

SEC. 13. That the lands acquired by the
agreements specified in the two preceding sections are hereby declared to be a part of the
public domain. Sections sixteen and thirty-
six in each township, whether surveyed or un-
surveyd, are hereby reserved from settlement
for the use and benefit of public schools, as provided in section ten relating to lands acquired
from the Cherokee Nation of Indians. And the
lands so acquired by the agreements specified
in the two preceding sections not so reserved
shall be opened to settlement by proclamation
of the President at the same time and in the
manner, and subject to the same conditions and
regulations provided in section ten relating to
the opening of the lands acquired from the
Cherokee Nation of Indians. And each settler

on the lands so to be opened as aforesaid shall, before receiving a patent for his homestead, pay to the United States for the land so taken by him, in addition to the fees provided by law, the sum of two dollars and fifty cents per acre; and shall also pay interest upon the amount so to be paid for said land from the date of entry to the date of final payment at the rate of four per centum per annum.

SEC. 14. Before any of the aforesaid lands are open to settlement it shall be the duty of the Secretary of the Interior to divide the same into counties, which shall contain as near as possible not less than five hundred square miles in each county. In establishing said county line the Secretary is hereby authorized to extend the lines of the counties already located so as to make the area of said counties equal, as near as may be, to the area of the counties provided for in this act. *Provided,* That range one west and ranges one, two, three and four east, in township twenty, shall be attacned to and become a part of Payne county. At the first election for county officers the people of each county may vote for a name for each county, and the name which receives the greatest number of votes shall be the name of such county. *Provided further,* That as soon as the county lines are designated by the Secretary he shall reserve not to exceed one-half section of land in each county, to be located for county seat purposes, to be entered under sections twenty-three hundred and eighty-seven and twenty-three hundred and eighty-eight of the Revised Statutes, and all reservations for county seats shall be specified in any order or proclamation which the President shall make for the opening of the lands to settlement.

SEC. 15. The consent of the United States is hereby given to the allotment of lands in severalty not exceeding one hundred and sixty acres to any one individual within the limits of the country occupied by the Cherokees, Creeks, Choctaws, Chicasaws and Seminoles; and upon such allotments the individuals to whom the same may be allotted shall be deemed to be in all respects citizens of the United States. And the sum of twenty-five thousand dollars, or so much thereof as may be necessary, is hereby appropriated to pay for the survey of any such lands as may be alloted by any of said tribes of Indians to individual members of said tribes; and upon the allotment of the lands held by said tribes respectively the reversionary interest of the U ited States therein shall be relinquished and shall cease.

SEC. 16. The President shall nominate and, by and with the advice and consent of the senate, shall appoint three commissioners to enter into negotiations with the Cherokee Nation, the Choctaw Nation, the Chicasaw Nation, the Muscogee (or Creek) Nation, the Seminole Nation, for the purpose of the extinguishment of the national or tribal title to any lands within that Territory now held by any and all of such nations or tribes, either by cession of the same or some part thereof to the United States, or by the allotment and division of the same in sev-

eralty amcng the Indians of such nations or
tribes respectively, as may be entitled to the
same, or by such other method as may be
agreed upon between the several nations and
tribes as aforesaid, or each of them, with the
United States, with the view to such an adjust-
ment, upon the basis of justice and equity, as
may, with the consent of such nations or tribes
of Indians, so far as may be necessary, be
requisite and suitable to enable the ultimate
creation of a state or states of the Union which
shall embrace the lands within said Indian Territory.

The commissioners so appointed shall each
receive a salary, to be paid during such time as
they may be actually employed, under direction of the President, in the duties enjoined by
this act, at the rate of five thousand dollars per
annum, and shall also be paid their reasonable
and proper expenses incurred in the prosecution of the objects of this act, upon accounts
therefor to be rendered to and allowed by the
Secretary of the Interior from time to time.
That such commissioners shall have power to
employ a secretary, a stenographer and such
interpretor or interpretors as may be found
necessary to the performance of their duties,
and by order to fix their compensation, which
shall be paid, upon the approval of the Secretary of the Interior, from time to time, with
their reasonable and necessary expenses, upon
accounts to be rendered as aforesaid; and may
also employ, in like manner and with the like
approval, a surveyor or other assistant or agent

which they shall certify in writing to be necessary to the performance of any part of their
duties.

Such commissioners shall, under such regulations and directions as shall be prescribed by
the President, through the Secretary of the Interior, enter upon negotiation with the several
nations of Indians as aforesaid in the Indian
Territory, and shall endeavor to procure, first,
such allotment of lands in severalty to the Indians belonging to each such nation, tribe or
band respectively, as may be agreed upon as
just and proper to provide for each such Indian
a sufficient quantity of land for his or her
needs, in such equal distribution and appor-
tionment as may be found just and suited to the
circumstances; for which purpose, after the
terms of such an agreement shall have been arrived at, the said commissioners shall cause the
land of any such nation or tribe or band to be
surveyed and the proper allotment to be designated; and, secondly, to procure the cession,
for such price and upon such terms as shall be
agreed upon, of any lands not found necessary
to be so allotted or divided, to the United
States; and to make proper agreements for the
investment or holding by the United States of
such moneys as may be paid or agreed to be
paid to such nation or tribes or bands, or to any
of the Indians thereof, for the extinguishment
of their interests therein. But said commissioners shall, however, have power to negotiate
any and all such agreements as, in view of all
the circumstances affecting the subject, shall be

found requisite and suitable to such an arrangement of the rights and interests and affairs of
such nations, tribes, bands of Indians, or any
of them, to enable the ultimate creation of a
Territory of the United States, with a view to
the admission of the same as a state in the
Union.

The commissioners shall at any time, or from
time to time, report to the Secretary of the Interior their transactions and the progress of
their negotiations, and shall at any time, or
from time to time, if separate agreements shall
be made by them with any nation, tribe or
band, in pursuance of the authority hereby conferred, report the same to the Secretary of the
Interior for submission to congress, for its consideration and ratification.

For the purposes aforesaid there is hereby
appropriated, out of any moneys in the treasury of the United States, the sum of fifty thous-
and dollars, to be immediately available.

Neither the provisions of this section nor the
negotiations or agreements which may be had
or made thereunder shall be held in any way
to waive or impair any right of sovereignty
which the government of the United States has
over or respecting said Indian Territory or the
people thereof, or any other right of the government relating to said, Territory, its lands or
the people thereof.

Approved March 3, 1893.

Section 13 of the Act of Congress approved
March 2, 1889, referred to in the above bill
reads as follows:

SEC. 13. That the lands acquired by the United States under said agreement shall be a part of the public domain, to be disposed of only as herein provided, and sections sixteen and thirty-six, of each township, whether surveyed or unsurveyed, are hereby reserved for the use and benefit of the public schools to be established within the limits of said lands under such conditions and regulations as may be hereafter enacted by Congress.

That the lands acquired by conveyance from the Seminole Indians hereunder, except the sixteenth and thirty-sixth sections, shall be disposed of to actual settlers under the homestead laws only, except as herein otherwise provided (except that section two thousand three hundred and one of the Revised Statutes shall not apply); *And provided further*, That any person who having attempted to, but for any cause failed, to secure a title in fee to a homestead under existing laws, or who made entry under what is known as the commuted provision of the homestead laws, shall be qualified to make a homestead entry upon said lands; *And provided further*, That the rights of honorably discharged Union soldiers and sailors in the late civil war as defined and described in sections twenty-three hundred and four and twenty-three hundred and five of the Revised Statutes shall not be abridged; *And provided further*, That each entry shall be in square form as nearly as practicable, and no person be permitted to enter more than one quarter section therof, but until said lands are opened for s⸌⸍

tlement by proclamation of the President, no person shall be permitted to enter upon and occupy the same, and no person violating this provision shall ever be permitted to enter any of said land or acquire any right thereto.

The Secretary of the Interior may, after said proclamation and not before, permit entry of said lands for townsites, under section twenty-three hundred and eighty-eight of the Revised Statutes, but no such entry shall embrace more than one half section of land.

Section 17 and 18 of the Act of March 3, 1891, referred to in the above bill and made a part thereof reads as follows.

SEC. 17. That before any lands in Oklahoma are opened to settlement it shall be the duty of the Secretary of the Interior to divide the same into counties which shall contain as near as possible not less than nine hundred square miles in each county. In establishing said county lines, the Secretary is hereby authorized to extend the lines of the counties already located so as to make the areas of said counties equal, as near as may be, to areas of the counties provided for in this act. At the first election for county officers the people of each county may vote for a name for each county, and the name which receives the greatest number of votes shall be the name of each county: *Provided further,* That as soon as the county lines are designated by the Secretary, he shall reserve not to exceed one half section of land in each county to be located near the center of said county for county seat purposes, **to** be entered under sections twenty-three hundred and eighty–seven and twenty-three hundred and eighty-eight of the Revised Statutes. *Provided*, That in addition to the jurisdiction granted to the Probate Courts and the judges thereof in Oklahoma Territory by legislative enactments which enactments are hereby ratified, the Probate Judges of said Territory are hereby granted such jurisdiction in townsite matters and under, such regulations as are provided by the laws of the State of Kansas. (Approved March 3, 1891.)

For jurisdiction of Probate Judge in townsite matters under statutes of Kansas, see index, "Kansas Statutes."

SEC. 18. That the school lands reserved in the Territory of Oklahoma by this and former acts of Congress may be leased for a period of not exceeding three years for the benefit of the school fund of said Territory by the Governor thereof, under regulations to be prescribed by the Secretary of the Interior.

Organic Act of Oklahoma.

(The Part Relating to Lands and Townsites.)

AN ACT to provide a temporary government for the Territory of Oklahoma, to enlarge the jurisdiction of the United States Court in the Indian Territory, and for other purposes. (Approved May 2, 1890.)

(This act is applicable to the Cherokee Outlet.)

Be it enacted by the Senate and House of Represe.ltatives of the United States of America, in Congress assembled!

*   *   *   *   *   *

School Lands,—SEC. 18.   That sections numbered sixteen and thirty-six in each township in said Territory shall be, and the same are hereby reserved for the purpose of being applied to the public schools of the state or states hereafter to be erected out of the same. In all cases where sections sixteen and thirty-six, or either of them, are occupied by actual settlers prior to survey thereof, the county commisioners of the counties in which such sections are so occupied are authorized to locate other lands to an equal amount, in sections or fractional sections, as the case may be, within their respective counties, in lieu of the sections so occupied.

Public Land Strip.—All the lands embraced in that portion of the Territory of Oklahoma known as the Public Land Strip shall be opened to settle-

ment under the provisions of the homestead, laws
of the United States, except section twenty-three
hundred and one of the Revised Statutes, which
shall not apply; but all actual and bona fide settlers upon and occupants of the land in said Public Land Strip at the time of the passage of this
act shall be entitled to have preference to and
hold the lands upon which they have settled under the homestead laws of the United States, by
virtue of their settlement and occupancy of said
lands, and they shall be credited with the time
they have actually occupied their homesteads, respectively, not exceeding two years, on the time
required under said laws to perfect title as homestead settlers.

The lands within said Territory of Oklahoma,
acquired by cession of the Muskogee (or Creek)
Nation of Indians, confirmed by act of congress
approved March first, eighteen hundred and
eighty-nine, and also the land acquired in pursuance of an agreement with the Seminole Nation
of Indians, by release and conveyance, dated
March sixteenth, eighteen hundred and eighty-
nine, which may hereafter be open to settlement,
shall be disposed of under the provisions of sections twelve, thirteen and fourteen of the "Act
making appropriations for the current and contingent expenses of the Indian Department, and for
fulfilling treaty stipulations with various Indian
tribes for the year ending June thirtieth, eighteen
hundred and ninety, and for other purposes," approved March second, eighteen hundred and
eighty-nine, and under section two of an "Act to

ratify and confirm an agreement with the Muskogee (or Creek) Nation of Indians in the Indian
Territory, and for other purposes," approved
March first, eighteen hundred and eighty-nine:
provided, however, that each settler under and in
accordance with the provisions of said acts shall,
before receiving a patent for his homestead on the
land hereafter opened to settlement as aforesaid,
pay to the United States for the land so taken by
him, in addition to the fee provided by law, the
sum of one dollar and twenty-five cents per acre.

Whenever any of the other lands within the
Territory of Oklahoma, now occupied by any Indian tribe, shall by operation of law or proclamation of the president of the United States, be open
to settlement, they shall be disposed of to actual
settlers only, under the provisions of the homestead law, except section twenty-three hundred and
one of the Revised Statutes of the United States,
which shall not apply: *Provided, however*, That
each settler, under and in accordance with the provisions of said homestead laws, shall before receiving a patent for his homestead, pay to the
United States for the the land so taken by him,
in addition to the fees provided by law, a sum per
acre equal to the amount which has been or may
be paid by the United States to obtain a relinquishment of the Indian title or interest therein,
but in no case shall such payment be less than one
dollar and twenty-five cents per acre. The rights
of honorably discharged soldiers and sailors in the
late civil war, as defined and described in sections
twenty-three hundred and four and twenty-three

hundred and five of the Revised Statutes of United States, shall not be abridged except as to such payment. All tracts of land in Oklahoma Territory which have been set apart for school purposes, to educational societies or missionary boards at work among the Indians, shall not be open for settlement, but are hereby granted to the respective educational societies or missionary boards for whose use the same has been set apart. No part of the land embraced within the Territory hereby created shall inure to the use and benefit of any railroad corporation, except the rights of way and lands heretofore granted to certain railroad corporations. Nor shall any provision of this act or any act of any officer of the United States, done or performed under the provisions of this act or otherwise, invest any corporation owning or operating any railroad in the Indian Territory, or territory created by this act, with any land or right to any land in either of said Territories, and this act shall not apply to or affect any land which, upon any condition on becoming a part of the public domain, would inure to the benegt of, or become the property of, any railroad corporation.

Land Office—Public Land Strip.—SEC. 19. That portion of the Territory of Oklahoma heretofore known as the Public Land Strip is hereby declared a public land district, and the President of the United States is hereby empowered to locate a land office in said district, at such a place as he shall select, and to appoint in conformity with existing law a register and receiver of said land office. He may also, whenever he shall deem it necessary, establish another additional land district within said Territory, locate a land office therein, and in like manner appoint a register and receiver thereof. And the commissioner of the general land office shall, when directed by the President, cause the lands within the Territory to be properly surveyed and subdivided where the same has not already been done.

Land Office Procedure.—SEC. 20. That the procedure in applications, entries, contests, adjudications in the Territory of Oklahoma shall be in form and manner prescribed under the homestead laws, except as modified by the provisions of this act and the acts of Congress approved March first and second, eighteen hundred and eighty-nine, heretofore mentioned, shall be applicable to all entries made in said Territory, but no patent shall be issued to any person who is not a citizen of the United States at the time of making final proof.

All persons who shall settle on land in said Territory, under the provisions of the homestead laws of the United States, and of this act, shall be required to select the same in square form as nearly as may be; and no person who shall at the time be seized in fee simple of a hundred and sixty acres of land in any State or Territory shall hereafter be entitled to enter land in said Territory of Oklahoma. The provisions of sections twenty-three hundred and four and twenty-three hundred and five of the Revised Statutes of the United States shall, except so far as modified by this act, apply to all homestead settlements in said Territory.

Commutation.—Sec. 21.   That any person entitled by law to take a homestead in said Territory of Oklahoma, who has already located and filed upon, or shall hereafter locate and file upon a homestead within the limits described in the President's proclamation of April first, eighteen hundred and eighty-nine, and under and in pursuance of the laws applicable to the settlement of the lands opened for settlement by such proclamation, and who has complied with all the laws relating to such homestead settlement, may receive patent therefor at the expiration of twelve months from the date of locating upon said homestead upon payment to the United States of one dollar and twenty-five cents per acre for land embraced in such homestead.

Sec. 22.   That the provisions of title thirty-two, chapter eight, of the Revised Statutes of the United States, relating to "reservation and sale of townsites on the public lands," shall apply to the lands open, or to be opened, to settlement in the Territory of Oklahoma, except those opened to settlement by the proclamation of the President on the twenty-second day of April, (March twenty-three), eighteen hundred and eighty-nine. *Provided*, that hereafter all surveys for townsites in said Territory shall contain reservations for parks (of substantially equal area, if more than one park), and for school and other public purposes, embracing in the aggregate not less than ten nor more than twenty acres: and patents for such reservations, to be maintained for such purposes, shall be issued to the towns respectively when organized as municipalities: *provided, further*, that in case any lands in said Territory of Oklahoma, which may be occupied and filed upon as a homestead, under the provisions of law applicable to said Territory, by a person who is entitled to perfect his title thereto under such laws, are required for townsite purposes, it shall be lawful for such person to apply to the Secretary of the Interior to purchase the lands embraced in said homestead, or any part thereof, for townsite purposes. He shall file with the application a plat of such proposed townsite, and if such plat be approved by the Secretary of the Interior, he shall issue a patent to such person, for land embraced in said townsite, upon the payment of the sum of ten dollars per acre for all the lands embraced in such townsite, except the lands to be donated and maintained for public purposes, as provided in this section. And the sums so received by the Secretary of the Interior shall be paid over to the proper authorities of the municipalities when organized, to be used by them for school purposes only.

Sec. 23. That there shall be reserved public highways four rods wide between each section of land in said Territory, the section lines being the center of said highways; but no deduction shall be made, where cash payments are provided for, in the amount to be paid for each quarter section of land by reason of such reservation. But if the said highway shall be vacated by any competent authority the title of the respective strips shall inure to the then owner of the tract of which it formed a part by the original survey.

SEC. 24. That it shall be unlawful for any person, for himself or any company, association or corporation, to directly or indirectly procure any person to settle upon any lands open to settlement in the Territory of Oklahoma, with intent thereafter of acquiring title thereto, and any title thus acquired shall be void; and the parties to such fraudulent settlement shall severally be guilty of a misdemeanor, and shall be punished upon indictment, by imprisonment not exceeding twelve months, or by a fine not exceeding one thousand dollars, or by both such fine and imprisonment, in the discretion of the court.

All of said acts are made a part of the Cherokee Outlet bill and applicable thereto, except so much thereof as may be in conflict with the provisions of said act.

Who May Take a Homestead.

The following qualifications are necessary for a person to take a homestead in the Cherokee Outlet, Tonkawa and Pawnee countries, as provided by Act of Congress approved March 3, 1893.

First, Every person who is the head of a family or who has arrived at the age of twenty-one years and is a citizen of the United States or who has filed his declaration to become such.

Second, No person who is the owner in fee simple of 160 acres of land in any State or Territory is entitled to enter a homestead in Oklahoma as provided in Section 20 of the Organic Act.

Third. The Act approved March 3, 1893, provides that any person who having attempted to, or for any cause failed to secure title in fee to a homestead under the existing laws or who made entry under what is known as the commuted provision of the homestead laws, shall be qualified to make homestead entry upon said lands.

FOURTH, Each entry must be in a square form as near as practicable and no person is permitted to enter more than one quarter section.

FIFTH, No person is permitted to occupy or enter upon any of these lands prior to the date fixed by the President opening the lands to homestead settlement. Under no circumstances whatever should a settler enter upon any of the lands until permitted to do so by the President's proclamation.

The head of a family includes a man under twenty-one years of age who is married. If a wife is divorced from or deserted by her husband so that she is dependent upon her own resources for support she then becomes the head of a family and can make homestead entry if otherwise qualified, whether she has arrived at the age of twenty-one years or not.

An unmarried woman who has arrived at the age of twenty-one years may make homestead entry.

The bill provides that soldiers and officers who have served in the army of the United States during the recent rebellion for a period of 90 days entitles them to make homestead entry without regard to age or citizenship, provided, that they are otherwise qualified. If the soldier be dead, his wife, or if she be dead, his minor heirs, by guardian duly appointed an! or dited at the Department at Washington, may make homestead entry.

An unmarried woman does not forfeit her homestead by marrying but must continue residence and cultivation on her homestead until final proof is made. Husband and wife while living together cannot hold two homestead claims.

A person may make his declaration to become a citizen of the United States before the Clerk of the District Court. A certified copy of the declaration of intention should be filed with the application to make homestead entry.

The bill opening the Cherokee Outlet to settlement provides that the President must give twenty days notice before the lands are opened to entry and settlement. This bill also provides that each settler on the lands before receiving a patent for his homestead must pay to the United States for the lands to be taken by him, in addition to the fees provided by law, the sum of $2.50 per acre for any land east of 97½ degrees west longitude, the sum of $1.50 per acre for any lands between 97½ degrees west longitude and 98½ degrees west longitude, the sum of $1.00 per acre for any lands west of 98½ degrees west longitude and shall also pay interest upon the amount so to be paid for said lands, from the date of entry to the date of final payment therefor, at the rate of 4 per cent per annum.

RIGHTS OF SOLDIERS AND SAILORS.

SECTIONS 2304 and 2305 are applicable to all soldiers and sailors who desire to take a homestead in the Cherokee Outlet, Tonkawa, Pawnee and Kickapoo countries and read as follows:

SEC. 2304 U. S. Statutes provides that every private soldier or officer, and every seaman, who served in the army of the United States, for ninety days, during the recent rebellion, and who was honorably discharged and has remained loyal to the government, shall be entitled to enter 160 acres of land, and he is allowed six months from time of filing his declaratory statement, to make his entry and commence his residence and improvements, and erect thereon a habitable dwelling.

SEC. 2305 Revised Statutes, provides that the time he served in the army shall be deducted from the time required under the homestead law to perfect title.

If a soldier was discharged on account of wounds received or disability incurred in the line of duty, then he is entitled to credit for the full term of his enlistment. In no case can he acquire title or patent, until he has resided upon, cultivated and improved the land for at least one year.

HOW TO TAKE A HOMESTEAD.

There are two ways in which a homestead may be taken.

FIRST. By actual settlement upon the land.

SECOND. By entry at the local United States Land Office.

An *actual settler* is one who goes upon the land with the intention of making it his home and does some act indicating his intention to appropriate the land to his own use and bene–

fit. This act of settlement must consist of some permanent and substantial improvement of a visible nature, so as to give notice to all persons that the land is taken in good faith and for the purpose of making a home thereof. An actual settler has three months in which to make his entry in the local Land Office and his right relates back to the date of settlement. A failure to make entry within three months from the settlement will open the land to the next claimant or settler who has complied with the law. No excuse will be accepted by the Department of the Interior for a failure on the part of the claimant or settler to make his entry at the Land Office within 90 days from the date of settlement where there is an adverse claimant, either by settlement on the land or by entry at the Land Office.

By the second method the homestead claimant may go directly to the United States Land Office in the district in which the land is situated and enter the land. As all of the lands in Oklahoma are declared to be non—mineral in character it is not necessary for the claimant to examine the land before making his entry. To make an entry it is necessary to file an application in the United States Land Office in the district where the land is situated, with affidavits showing his qualifications to make homestead entry and pay the fees and commissions, which in Oklahoma are for 160 acres, $14.00, for 80 acres, $7.00, for 40 acres, $6.00.

Where two persons have initiated a homestead right to the same tract of land, one by settlement upon the land and the other by entry at the Land Office, the first in point of time will hold the land.

It is very important that all papers should be correctly drawn. A mistake in the discription of land will make you endless trouble and finally cause you the loss of your home.

RESIDENCE.

The following general regulations are applicable to persons establishing residence upon a homestead.

FIRST. Residence upon a homestead must be in person and cannot be delegated to any one else.

SECOND. The period of continuous residence begins from the date of the entry at the Land Office or at the date of actual settlement upon the land.

THIRD. A party who temporarily leaves his homestead to care for other property does not abandon his residence thereon.

FOURTH. The fact that a homesteader sometimes slept upon and ate upon the land is not regarded as sufficient compliance with the law.

FIFTH. Residence cannot be claimed on the tract during the time it was covered by another homestead entry.

SIXTH. The refusal of the wife to live on the homestead, provided, the husband complies with the law will not affect his rights.

SEVENTH. Where failure to comply with the law results from causes beyond the reasonable control of the claimant his entry will not be cancelled if the facts can be duly proved.

EIGHTH. Threats or other acts of violence will excuse failure to maintain residence. However, these threats must be of such a nature as are calculated to operate upon persons of ordinary firmness so as to cause apprehension of loss of life or great bodily injury.

NINTH. The Act of May 2, 1892, which is the Organic Act of Oklahoma having been made applicable to the opening of the Cherokee Outlet, title may be acquired to these lands *after 12 months actual residence and payment of money as provided in said act.*

But it must be remembered that all persons are required to make a cash payment for the lands besides the fees and commissions as provided in the act opening said lands to settlement and the only advantage a soldier or sailor has over other parties seeking to take a claim, is that, he may file his declaratory statement in person, or by some duly authorized agent.

A soldier in filing a declaratory statement, either in person or by his duly authorized agent must also file the original or certified copy of his discharge. In the event that the discharge or certified copy thereof cannot be produced the soldier should make his own affidavit showing his service in the army and corroborated by two witnesses. However, if it is satisfactorily shown that the witnesses cannot be produced then the soldier's own affidavit will be sufficient.

A soldier in filing his declaratory statement by himself or duly authorized agent exhausts his homestead right the same as in filing a regular homestead entry.

A soldier or sailor must within six months after filing a declaratory statement by himself or duly appointed agent, make his final entry at the local United States Land Office where his declaratory statement was made by himself or his duly appointed agent, and establish his residence upon the land. A failure to comply with any of these regulations will work a forfeiture of his land where there is any other claimant.

Any person who has filed a declaratory statement prior to March 2, 1889, and failed, for any cause to secure title in fee simple thereunder, has the right to make another declaratory statement and entry in any of the above lands.

FORMS.

HOMESTEAD.

APPLICATION }
NO . . . . }   LAND OFFICE AT . . . .
. . . . 189 . . .

I, ... , of . . . .
. . . . do hereby apply to enter,
under section 2289, Revised Statutes of the
United States, the . . . . of Section . . . .
in Township . . . . of Range . . . .
containing . . . . acres.

. . . .

LAND OFFICE AT. . . . .
. . . . 18 . . . .

I, ... Register of the Land
Office, de her__, _ertify that the above applica-
tion is for surveyed lands of the class which the
applicant is legally entitled to enter under section 2289, Revised Statutes of the United States,
and that there is no prior valid adverse right to
the same.

. . . .

Register.

HOMESTEAD AFFIDAVIT.
LAND OFFICE AT . . . .
. . . . 189 . . . . .
. . . . of . . . . ,

having filed my application No......... ....,for an
entry under section 2289, Revised Statutes of
the United States, do solemny swear that I am
not the owner in fee simple of one hundred and
sixty acres of land in any State or Territory;
that I am *..

[Here insert statement that affiant is a citizen
of the United States, or that he has filed his
declaration of 'intention to become such, and
that he is the head of a family, or is over twenty-
one years of age, as the case may be. It should
be stated whether applicant is *native-born* or
not, and if not a certified copy of his certificate
of naturalization, or declaration of intention, as
the case may be, must be furnished.]

....

that my said application is honestly and in good
faith made for the purpose of actual settlement
and cultivation, and not for the benefit of any
other person, persons, or corporation, and that
I will faithfully and honestly endeavor to comply with all the requirements of law as to settlement, residence, and cultivation necessary to
acquire title to the land applied for; that I am
not acting as agent of any person, corporation,
or syndicate in making such entry, nor in collusion with any person, corporation, or syndicate
to give them the benefit of the land entered, or
any part thereof, or the timber thereon; that I
do not apply to enter the same for the purpose
of speculation, but in good faith to obtain a
home for myself, and that I have not directly
or indirectly made, and will not make, any agreement or contract in any way or manner, with

any person or persons, corporation or syndicate whatsoever, by which the title which I might acquire from the government of the United States should inure in whole or in part to the benefit of any person except myself, and further, that since August 30, 1890, I have not entered under the land laws of the United States, or filed upon, a quantity of land, agricultural in character, and not mineral, which, with the tracts now applied for, would make more than three hundred and twenty acres.

[Here add an exception, if any, of land settled upon prior to August 30, 1890, giving date of settlement commenced, and describing improvements, and that the party has not heretofore made any entry under the homestead laws.]

Sworn to and subscribed before me this.............. day of......................... 189.......

AFFIDAVIT.

LAND OFFICE AT............... ....

(Date)......................................, 18......

I, ..., of.............................., applying to enter (or file for) a homestead, do solemnly swear that I did not enter upon and occupy any portion of the lands described and declared open to entry in the President's proclamation dated March 23, 1889, prior to 12 o'clock, noon, of April 22, 1889.

Sworn to and subscribed before me this ....day of......................................., 18.......

NOTE—In making entries in the new lands to be opened, the date on which the said lands were opened must be substituted for dates in above affidavit.

SOLDIERS' POWER OF ATTORNEY.

I, ..., of............................ County, and State or Territory of............................' do solemnly swear that I served for a period of ....in the army of the United States during the war of the rebellion, and was honorably discharged therefrom, as shown by a statement of such service herewith, and that I have remained loyal to the government; that I have never made homestead entry or filed a declaratory statement under sections 2290, 2304, or 2309 of the Revised Statutes; ....I do hereby appoint ...., of............................County, and State of........................ ..., my true and lawful agent, under Section 2309 aforesaid, to select for me and in my name, and file my declaratory statement for a homestead under the aforesaid sections; and I hereby give notice of my intention to claim and enter said tract under said statute; that my said attorney has no interest, present or prospective, in the premises, and that I have made no arrangement or agreement with him or any other person for any sale or attempted sale or relinquishment of my claim in any manner or for any consideration whatever, and that I have not signed thia declaration in blank, that I am not the proprietor of more than one hundred and sixty acres of land in any State or Territory, that my said application is honestly and in good faith made for the purpose of actual settlement and cultivation, and not for the benefit of any other person, persons, or corporation, and that I will faithfully and honestly endeavor to comply with all the requirements of law, as to settlement, residence, and cultivation necessary to acquire title to the land applied for; that I am not acting as agent of any person, corporation, or syndicate, in making such entry, nor in collusion with any person, corporation. or syndicate to give them the benefit of the land entered, or any part thereof, or the timber thereon, that I do not apply to enter the same for the purpose of speculation, but in good faith to obtain a home for myself, that I have not directly or indirectly made and will not make any agreement or contract in any way or manner, with any person or persons, corporation or syndicate whatsoever, by which the title which I might acquire from the government of the United States should inure in whole or in part to the benefit of any person except myself: and further, that since August 30, 1890, I have not entered under the land laws of the United States, or filed upon, a quantity of land, agricultural in character and not mineral, which, with the tracts no applied for, would make more than three hundred and twenty acres. (Here add an exception, if any, of land settled upon prior to August 30, 1890, giving date of settlement commenced, and describing improvements.)

Acknowledged, sworn to and subscribed before me this................day of............................189...., and I certify that the foregoing declaration was fully filled out before being subscribed or attested.

$\{$ OFFICIAL SEAL. $\}$ ....

ATTORNEY'S STATEMENT.

By virtue of the foregoing, and of a certain power of attorney therein named, duly executed on the........day of..........and filed herewith, I hereby select the.....................................
.. ..as the homestead claim of ...., the aforesaid, and do solemnly swear that the same is filed in good faith for the purpose therein specified, and that I have no interest or authority in the matter, present or prospective, beyond the filing of the same as the true and lawful agent of the said................................ , as provided by Section 2209 of the Revised Statutes of the United States.

....Agent.

Sworn and subscribed before me this............... day of............................189...
$\{$ OFFICIAL SEAL. $\}$ ....
NOTE.—This form may be used where the de-

claratory statement is filed by an agent under Section 2309, Revised Statutes.

SOLDIER'S DECLARATORY STATEMENT

[This is the old authorized form, but should be amended to correspond with new affidavit required of homestead entrymen under act of March 3, 1891.   See homestead affidavit.]

I, ...of.. County and State or Territory of............................... do solemnly swear that I served for a period of ....in the army of the United States during the war of the rebellion, and was honorably discharged therefrom, as shown by a statement of such service herewith, and that I have remained loyal to the government; that I have never made homestead entry or filed a de- claratory statement under Sections 2290 and 2304 of the Revised Statutes; that I have located as a homestead under said statute the..................... ....and hereby give notice of my intention to claim and enter said tract; that this location is made for my exclusive use and ben- efit, for the purpose of my actual settlement and cultivation, and not either directly or indirectly for the use or benefit of any other person.

My present postoffice address is...............................

....

Sworn to and subscribed before me this............ day of...18....... [SEAL.]   .... NOTE.—This form may be used where the soldier files his own declaratory statement.

APPLICATION TO LEASE SCHOOL LAND.

To William C. Remfrow, Governor of Oklahoma, Guthrie O. T.

Sir:

I,..........................of................ hereby apply to lease: under the Thirty-sixth Section of the Act of Congress, Approved March 3d. 1891, and the regulations prescribed by the Secretary of the Interior, the following described tract of school land in............. ....County Oklahoma Territory to-wit: ....of school section........ township............north of range......:... (east or west) of the Indian Meridian, for the term of.... ....not exceeding three years from the first day of February. 189..for which I hereby agree to pay an annual rental of ....Dollars per quarter section to be paid as follows:. ....dollars cash upon execution of lease by lessee,........ ....Dollars December 15, 189...., ...Dollars December 15 189....by notes with approved personal security.

The following is a description of the natural character of said land; ....

The following is a description of the improvements on said land and cultivation thereof;.... ....

....
....
....
Made by............................
     (Signed) ......\.........
        P. O. ....
           County...........
            Territory of Oklahoma.
Dated................189....

INSTRUCTIONS TO APPLICANTS.

1 Write proper names distinctly and in full.

2 The lease year begins on the first day of February of each year and the lease cannot be made for a longer period than three years from said date.

3 All leases executed by lessees prior to November first will be dated back to the first day of February preceding but rent will be charged only from the date of execution of the lease by lessee.

4 It is imperative that approved personal security be given on all notes.

5 Personal checks will not be received.

SCHOOL LAND LEASE

This Indenture made by and between Wm. C. Renfrow as Governor of the Territory of Oklahoma, of the first part, and...........
....
...............of the second part, witnesseth,

That the said party of the first part, by virtue of the authority vested in him by the thirty-sixth section of the act of Congress approved March 3d, 1891, and the regulations prescribed

by the Secretary of the Interior, therein provided for, and in consideration of the covenants of
the said party of the second part hereinafter set
forth, has this day leased to the said party of
the second part. the following described School
land, to-wit: The................of section
.... Township ....
North, of range......................of the
Indian Meridian in ....
Couı ty ,Oklahoma Territory, to have and to
hold the same for the term of............years
from the first day of February, 189...., for
which said party of the second part hereby
agrees to pay therefor the sum of ....
....dollars,
cash in hand, the receipt whereof is hereby
acknowledged.......................... ...dollars
on the 15th day of December, 189...., and
....dollars
on the 15th day of December, 189 ....and....
....dollars,
on this 15th day of December, 189....

The said deferred payments are evidenced by
...........certain joint, several, promissory
notes of even date herewith, signed by the said
party of the second part and ....

....

for the above amounts, due and payable at the
times above set forth.

The said party of the second part covenants
with the said party of the first part, that he will
not cut or remove, or permit to be cut or removed, any timber from said land, that he will
not quarry or remove, or permit to be quarried

or removed, any building or other stone from said land, except such as may be necessary for the foundations for building thereon; that he will not mine or remove, or permit to be mined or removed, any minerals therefrom; that he is leasing said land for agricultural and grazing purposes, and that he will cultivate the same in a husbandman-like manner; that he will not assign this lease, nor underlet any portion of the leased premises, and that he will not commit any acts of waste upon or to said land.

It is further agreed by and between the parties of this lease that the said party of the second part may at the expiration of the time for which this lease is made, remove any or all of the improvements he may have placed upon said land, unless the said party of the second part shall be in default for payment of said rental, or a part thereof, or has violated any of the conditions herein.

If default is made in the payment of said rental, or the conditions of this lease have been violated, the improvements upon said land, and the growing crops thereon, shall not be removed by the said party of the second part, or any one claiming under him, until such rental has been fully paid, to-gether with interest, costs, damages, and attorney fees arising from the violation of the conditions of this lease, and such unpaid rental, interest, costs, damages and attorney fees as aforesaid, shall become a lien upon the improvements on said land, and the growing crops thereon, and such improvements or growing crops may be sold at public or pri-

v
hate sale by the said party of the first part, or
is successor in office, without notice to the
said party of the second part, and the proceeds
of such sale applied to the satisfaction of the
unpaid part of said rental, and in satisfaction
of the damages, interest, costs, and attorney
fees, as aforesaid.

It is hereby expressly understood by and between the parties to this lease, that upon the
nonpayment of said rental or any part thereof
at the time the same shall become due and payable, or upon the failure or refusal of the said
party of the second part to furnish additional
security for any deferred payments, when requested so to do by the said party of the first
part, or his successor in office, or if the said
party of the second part shall fail, in any manner to comply with the provisions of this lease,
or violates any of the conditions thereof, the
said party of the first part, or his successor in
office, may. at his option, declare this lease forfeited, and the said party of the first part, or
any other person lawfully entitled to the possession thereof, on behalf of, or representing the
United States, shall have the right to take immediate and peaceable possession of said premises, together with the improvements and
growing crops thereon situated. And upon the
termination of this lease, either by the expiration of the time for which this lease is made,
or by reason of the violations of any of the conditions hereinbefore set forth, any instrument in
writing signed by the said party of the first part

cr his successor in office, showing that the person or officer named therein is entitled to the possession of the land, or that he takes possession of the improvements and growing crops thereon on behalf of the United States, shall be sufficient authority for such person or officer, to take possession of the land, and to take possession of and sell the improvements and growing crops thereon, for the purpose of paying any part of said rental due and unpaid, with interest, costs, damages and attorney fees as hereinbefore provided for.

If the party of the second part desires to re-lease said land at the expiration of the time for which this lease is made and files his application therefor with the said party of the first part, or his successor in office, on or before the first day of........................189.....and has complied with all the conditions herein, he will be given a preference to release said land at the highest acceptable rental offered by any responsible bidder, but the right is reserved by the said party of the first part to reject all bids.

If at any time after the execution of this lease it is shown to the the party of the first part, or his successor in office, that there has been any fraud or collusion upon the part of the said party of the second part to obtain this lease at a less rental than its value, it shall be null and void at the option of the party of the first part.

This lease is made and accepted subject to the approval of the Secretary of the Interior and to any prior rights existing in favor of the Indians.

Witness the hands and seals of the parties aforesaid, this....day of............, 189..

Witness: ....(Seal.)
                                          Governor.

....(Seal.)

...............,

    Approved

....

    Secretary of the Interior.

RULES OF PRACTICE.

I.

(Proceedings before Registers and Receivers.)

1.—Initiation of Contests.

Rule 1.—Contest may be initiated by an adverse party or other person against a party to any entry, filing, or other claim under laws of congress relating to the public lands, for any sufficient cause affecting the legality or validity of the claim.

Rule 2.—In every case of application for a hearing an affidavit must be filed by the contestant with the register and receiver, fully setting forth the facts which constitute the grounds of contest.

Rule 3.—Where an entry has been allowed and remains of record the affidavit of the contestant must be accompanied by the affidavit of one or more witnesses in support of the allegations made.

2.—Hearing in Contested Cases.

Rule 4.—Registers and receivers may order hearings in all cases wherein entry has not been perfected and no certificate has been issued as a basis for patent.

Rule 5.—In case of an entry or location on which final certificate has been issued the hearing will be ordered only by direction of the commissioner of the general land office.

Rule 6.—Applications for hearings under

rule 5 must be transmitted by the register and receiver, with special report and recommendation, to the commissioner, for his determination and instructions.

3.—*Notice of Contest.*

Rule 7.—At least thirty days notice shall be given of all hearings before the register and receiver, unless by written consent an earlier day shall be agreed upon.

Rule 8.—The notice of contest and hearing must conform to the following requirements:

1. It must be written or printed.

2. It must be signed by the register and receiver, or one of them.

3. It must state the time and place of hearing.

4. It must describe the land involved.

5. It must state the register and receiver's number of the entry and the land office where, and the date when made, and the name of the party making the same.

6. It must give the name of the contestant, and briefly state the grounds and purpose of the contest.

7. It may contain any other information pertinent to the contest.

4.—*Service of Notice.*

Rule 9.—Personal service shall be made in all cases when possible if the party to be served is a resident in the state or territory in which the land is situated, and shall consist in the delivery of a copy of the notice to each person to be served.

Rule 10.—Personal service may be executed by any officer or person.

Rule 11.—Notice may be given by publication only when it is shown by affidavit of the contestant, and by such other evidence as the register and receiver may require, that due diligence has been used and that personal service cannot be made. The party will be required to state what effort has been made to get personal service.

Rule 12.—When it is found that the prescribed service cannot be had, either personal or by publication, in time for the hearing provided for in the notice, the notice may be returned prior to the time fixed for the hearing, and a new notice issued fixing another time of hearing, for the proper service thereof, an affidavit being filed by the contestant showing due diligence and inability to serve the notice in time.

5.—*Notice by Publication.*

Rule 13.—Notice by publication shall be made by advertising the notice at least once a week for four successive weeks in some newspaper published in the county wherein the land in contest lies; and if no newspaper be published in such county, then in the newspaper published in the county nearest to such land. The first insertion shall be at least thirty days prior to the day fixed for the hearing.

Rule 14.—Where notice is given by publication, a copy of the notice shall be mailed by registered letter to the last known address of each person to be notified thirty days before date of hearing, and a like copy shall be posted in the register's office during the period of publication, and also in a conspicuous place on the land, for at least two weeks prior to the day set for hearing.

6.—*Proof of Service of Notice.*

Rule 15.—Proof of personal service shall be the written acknowledgement of the person served or the affidavit of the person who served the notice attached thereto, stating the time, place, and manner of service.

Rule 16.—When service is by publication, the proof of service shall be a copy of the advertisement, with the affidavit of the publisher or foreman attached thereto, showing that the same was successively inserted the requisite number of times, and the date thereof.

7.—*Notice of Interlocutory Proceedings.*

Rule 17.—Notice of interlocutory motions, proceedings, orders and decisions shall be in writing, and may be served personally or by registered letter through the mail to the last known address of the party.

Rule 18.—Proof of service by mail shall be the affidavit of the person who mailed the notice, attached to the postoffice receipt for the registered letter.

8.—*Rehearings.*

Rule 19.—Orders for re-hearing must be brought to the notice of the parties in the same manner as in case of original proceedings.

9.—*Continuances.*

Rule 20.—A postponement of a hearing to a day to be fixed by the register and receiver may be allowed on the day of trial on account of the absence of material witnesses, when the party asking for the continuance makes an affidavit before the register and receiver showing:

1. That one or more of the witnesses in his behalf is absent without his procurement or consent;

2. The name and residence of each witness;

3. The facts to which they would testify if present;

4. The materiality of the evidence;

5. The exercise of proper diligence to procure the attendance of the absent witnesses; and

6. That affiant believes said witnesses can be had at the time to which it is sought to have the trial postponed.

7. Where hearings are ordered by the commissioner of the general land office in cases to which the United States is a party, continuances will be granted in accordance with the usual practice in United States cases in the courts, without requiring an affidavit on the part of the government.

Rule 21.—One continuance only shall be allowed to either party on account of absent witnesses, unless the party applying for a further continuance shall at the same time apply for an order to take the depositions of the alleged absent witnesses.

Rule 22.—No continuance shall be granted when the opposite party shall admit that the witnesses would, if present, testify to the statement set out in the application for continuance.

10.—Depositions on Interrogatories.

Rule 23.—Testimony may be taken by deposition in the following cases:

1. Where the witness is unable, from age, infirmity, or sickness, or shall refuse to attend the hearing at the local land office.

2. Where the witness resides more than fifty miles from the place of trial, computing distance by the usual traveled route.

3. Where the witness resides out or is about to leave the state or territory, or is absent therefrom.

4. Where from any cause it is apprehended that the witness may be unable or will refuse to attend, in which case the deposition will be used only in event that the personal attendance of the witness cannot be obtained.

Rule 24.—The party desiring to take a deposition under Rule 23 must comply wilh the following regulations:

1. He must make affidavit before the register or receiver, setting forth one or more of the

above named causes for taking such deposition, and that the witness is material.

2. He must file with the register and receiver the interrogatories to be propounded to the witness.

3. He must state the name and residence of the witness.

4. He must serve a copy of the interrogatories on the opposing party or his attorney.

Rule 25.—The opposing party will be allowed ten days in which to file cross-interrogatories.

Rule 26.—After the expiration of the ten days allowed for filing cross-interrogatories a commission to take the deposition shall be issued by the register and receiver, which commission shall be accompanied by a copy of all the interrogatories filed.

Rule 27.—The register and receiver may designate any officer authorized to administer oaths within the county or district where the witness resides to take such deposition.

Rule 28.—It is the duty of the officer before whom the deposition is taken to cause the interrogatories appended to the commission to be written out and the answer thereto to be inserted immediately underneath the respective questions, and the whole, when completed, to be read over to the witness, and must be by him subscribed and sworn to in the usual manner before the witness is discharged.

Rule 29.—The officer must attach his certificate to the deposition, stating that the same was subscribed and sworn to by the deponent at the time and place therein mentioned.

Rule 30.—The deposition and certificate, together with the commission and interrogatories, must then be sealed up, the title of the cause indorsed on the envelope, and the whole returned by mail or express to the register and receiver.

Rule 31.—Upon receipt of the package at the local land office, the date when the same is opened must be indorsed on the envelope and the body of the deposition by the local land officers.

Rule 32.—If the officer designated to take the deposition has no official seal, a proper certificate of his official character, under seal, must accompany his return.

Rule 33.—The parties in any case may stipulate in writing to take depositions before any qualified officer, and in any manner.

Rule 34.—All stipulations by parties or counsel must be in writing, and be filed with the register and receiver.

11.—Oral Testimony Before Other Officers than Registers and Receivers.

Rule 35.—In the discretion of registers, testimony may be taken near the land in controversy before a United States commissioner or other officer authorized to administer oaths, at a time and place fixed by them and stated in the notice of hearing.

2. Officers taking testimony under the foregoing rule will be governed by the rules applicable to trials before registers and receivers. (See Rules 36 to 42, inclusive.)

3. Testimony so taken must be certified to, sealed up and transmitted by mail or express to the register and receiver, and the receipt thereof at the local office noted on the papers, in the same manner as provided in case of depositions by Rules 29 to 32, inclusive.

4. On the day set for hearing at the local office the register and receiver will examine the testimony taken by the officer designated, and render a decision thereon in the same manner as if the testimony had been taken before themselves. (See Rules 50 to 53, inclusive.)

5. No charge for examining testimony in such cases will be made by the register and receiver.

6. Officers designated to take testimony under this rule will be allowed to charge such fees as are properly authorized by the tariff of fees existing in the local courts of their respective districts, to be taxed in the same or equivalent manner as costs are taxed by registers and receivers under Rules 54 to 58, inclusive.

7. When an officer designated to take testimony under this rule, or when an officer designated to take depositions, under Rule 27, cannot act on the day fixed for taking testimony or deposition, the testimony or deposition, as the case may be, will be deemed properly taken before any other qualified officer at the same

place and time, who may be authorized by the officer originally designated, or by agreement of parties, to act in the place of the officer first named.

12.—Trials.

Rule 36.—Upon the trial of a cause the register and receiver may in any case, and should in all cases when necessary, personally direct the examination of the witnesses, in order to draw from them facts within their knowledge requsite to a correct conclusion by the officer, upon any point connected with the case.

Rule 37.—The register and receiver will be careful to reach, if possible, the exact condition and status of the land involved by any contest, and will ascertain all the facts having any bearing upon the rights of parties in interest.

Rule 38.—In pre-emption cases they will particularly ascertain the nature, extent, and value of alleged improvements; by whom made, and when; the true date of the settlement of persons claiming: the steps taken to mark and secure the claim, and the exact status of the land at that date as shown upon the records of their office.

Rule 39.—In like manner, under the homestead and other laws, the conditions affecting the inception of the alleged right, as well as the subsequent acts of the respective claimants, must be fully and specifically examined.

Rule 40.—Due opportunity will be allowed opposing claimants to confront and cross–

examine the witnesses introduced by either party.

Rule 41.—No testimony will be excluded from the record by the register and receiver on the ground of any objection thereto; but when objection is made to testimony offered, the exceptions will be noted, and the testimony, with the exceptions, will come up with the case for the consideration of the commissioner. Officers taking testimony will, however, summarily put a stop to obviously irrelevant questioning.

Rule 42.—Upon the day originally set for hearing, and upon any day to which the trial may be continued, the testimony of all the witnesses present shall be taken and reduced to writing. When testimony is taken in shorthand, the stenographer's notes must be written out, and the written testimony then and there subscribed by the witness and testified by the officer before whom the same is taken.

13.—Appeals.

Rule 43.—Appeals from the final action or decisions of registers and receivers lie in every case to the commissioner of the general land office. (Revised Statutes, sections 453, 2478.)

Rule 44.—After hearing in a contested case has been had and closed, the register and receiver will, in writing, notify the parties in interest of the conclusions to which they have arrived, and that thirty days are allowed for an appeal from their decision to the commissioner, the notice to be served personally or by registered letter through the mail to their last known address.

Rule 45.—The appeal must be in writing or in print, and should set forth in brief and clear terms the specific points of exception to the ruling appealed from.

Rule 46.—Notice of appeal and copy of specification of errors shall be served on appellee within the time allowed for appeal, and appellee shall be allowed ten days for reply before transmittal of the record to the goneral land office.

Rule 47.—No appeal from the action or decisions of the register and receiver will be received at the general land office unless forwarded through the local officers.

Rule 48.—In case of a failure to appeal from the decision of the local officers, their decision will be considered final as to the facts in the case, and will be disturbed by the commissioner only as follows:

1. Where fraud or gross irregularity is suggested on the face of the papers.

2. Where the decision is contrary to existing laws or regulations.

3. In event of disagreeing decisions by the local officers.

4. Where it is not shown that the party against whom the decision was rendered was duly notified of the decision and of his right of appeal.

Rule 49.—In any of the foregoing cases the commissioner will reverse or modify the decision of the local officers or remand the case, at his discretion.

Rule 50.—All documents once received by the local officers must be kept on file with the cases, and the date of filing must be noted thereon; and no papers will be allowed, under any circumstances, to be removed from the files or taken from the custody of the register and receiver, but access to the same, under proper rules, so as not to interfere with necessary public business, will be permitted to the parties in interest, or their attorneys, under the supervision of those officers.

14.—*Reports and Opinions.*

Rule 51.—Upon the termination of a contest the register and receiver will render a joint report and opinion in the case, making full and specific reference to the postings and annotations upon their records.

Rule 52.—The register and receiver will promptly forward their report, together with the testimony and all the papers in the case, to the commissioner of the general land office, with a brief letter of transmittal, describing the case by its title, the nature of the contest, and the tract involved.

Rule 53.—The local officers will thereafter take no further action affecting the disposal of the land in contest until instructed by the commissioner.

15.—*Taxation of Costs.*

Rule 54.—Parties contesting pre-emption, homestead, or timber-culture entries and claiming preference rights of entry under second section of the act of May 14, 1880, (21 Stat. 140), must pay the costs of contest.

Rule 55.—In other contested cases each party must pay the costs of taking testimony upon his own direct and cross-examination.

Rule 56.—The accumulation of excessive costs under Rule 54 will not be permitted; but where the officer taking testimony shall rule that a course of examination is irrelevant, and check the same under Rule 41, he may, nevertheless, in his discretion, allow the same to proceed at the sole cost of the party making such examination.

Rule 57.—Where parties contesting pre-emption, homestead, or timber-culture entries establish their right of entry under the pre-emption or homestead laws of the land in contest by virtue of actual settlement and improvement, without reference to the act of May 14, 1880, the cost of contest will be adjudged under Rule 55.

Rule 58.—Registers and receivers will apportion the costs of contest in accordance with the foregoing rules, and may require the party liable thereto to give security in advance of trial, by deposit or otherwise, in a reasonable sum or sums, for payment of the costs of transcribing the testimony.

Rule 59.—-The costs of contest chargeable

by registers and receivers are the legal fees for reducing testimony to writing. No other contest fees or costs will be allowed to or charged by those officers, directly or indirectly.

Rule 60.—Contestants must give their own notices and pay the expenses thereof.

Rule 61—Upon the termination of a trial, any excess in the sum deposited as security for costs of transcribing the testimony will be returned to the proper party.

Rule 62.—When hearings are ordered by the commissioner by the Secretary of the Interior, upon the discovery of reasons for suspension in the usual course of examination of entries, the preliminary costs will be provided from the contingent fund for the expenses of local land offices.

Rule 63.—The preliminary costs provided for by the preceding section will be collected by the register and receiver when the parties are brought before them in obedience to the order of hearing.

Rule 64.—The register and receiver will then require proper provision to be made for such further notification as may become necessary in the usual progress of the case to final decision.

Rule 65.—The register and receiver will append to their report in each case a statement of costs and the amount actually paid by each of the contestants, and also a statement of the amount deposited to secure the payment of the costs, how said sum was apportioned, and the amount returned, if any, and to whom.

16—*Appeals jrom Decisions Rejecting Applications to Enter Public Lands.*

Rule 66.—For the purpose of enabling appeals to be taken from the rulings or action of the local officers relative to applications to file upon, enter, or locate the public lands, the following rules will be observed:

1. The register and receiver will indorse upon every rejected application the date when presented and their reasons for rejecting it.

2. They will promptly advise the party in interest of their action, and of his right of appeal to the commissioner.

3. They will note upon their records a memorandum of the transaction.

Rule 67.—The party aggrieved will be allowed thirty days from receipt of notice in which to file his appeal in the local land office. Where the notice is sent by mail, five days additional will be allowed for the transmission of notice and five for the return of the appeal.

Rule 68.—The register and receiver will promptly forward the appeal to the general land office, together with a full report upon the case.

Rule 69.—This report should recite all the facts and the proceedings had, and must embrace the following particulars:

1. A statement of the application and rejection, with the reasons for rejection.

2. A description of the tract involved and a statement of its status, as shown by the records of the local land office.

3. References to all entries, filings, annotations, memoranda, and correspondence shown by the records relating to said tract and to the proceedings had.

Rule 70.—Rules 43 to 48, inclusive, and rule 93 are applicable to all appeals from the decisions of registers and receivers.

II.

(Proceedings before Surveyors-General.)

Rule 71.—The proceedings in hearings and contests before surveyor-general shall, as to notices, depositions, and other matters, be governed as nearly as may be by the rules prescribed for proceedings before registers and receivers, unless otherwise provided by law.

III.

(Proceedings before the Commissioner of the General Land Office and Secretary of the Interior.)

I.—Examination and Argument.

Rule 72.—When a contest has been closed before the local land officers and their report forwarded to the general land office, no additional evidence will be admitted in the case, unless offered under stipulation of the parties to the record, except where such evidence is presented as the basis of a motion for a new trial or in support of a mineral application or protest; but this rule will not prevent the commissioner, in the exercise of his discretion, from ordering further investigation when necessary.

Rule 73.—After the commissioner shall have received a record of testimony in a contest case, thirty days will be allowed to expire before any action thereon is taken, unless, in the judgment of the commissioner, public policy or private necessity shall demand summary action, in which case he will proceed at his discretion, first notifying the attorneys of record of his proposed action.

Rule 74.—When a case is pending on appeal from the decision of the register and receiver or surveyor-general, and argument is not filed before the same is reached in its order for examination, the argument will be considered closed, and thereafter no further arguments or motions of any kind will be entertained except upon written stipulation, duly filed, or good cause shown to the commissioner.

Rule 75.—If before decision by the commissioner either party should desire to discuss a case orally, reasonable opportunity therefor will be given in the discretion of the commissioner, but only at a time to be fixed by him upon notice to the opposing counsel, stating time and specific points upon which discussion is desired; and, except as herein provided, no oral hearings or suggestions will be allowed.

2.—Hearing and Review.

Rule 79.—Motions for rehearing before registers and receivers, or for review or consideration of the decisions of the commissioner or ecretary, will be allowed, in accordance with egal principles to motions for new trials at law, after due notice to the opposing party.

Rule 77.—Motions for rehearing and review, except as provided in Rule 114, must be filed in the office wherein the decision to be affected by such hearing or review was made, or in the local land office, for transmittal to the general land office; and, except when based upon newly discovered evidence, must be filed within thirty days from notice of such decision.

Rule 78.—Motions for rehearing and review must be accompanied by an affidavit of the party, or his attorney, that the motion is made in good faith, and not for the purpose of delay.

Rule 79.—The time between the filing of a motion for rehearing or review and the notice of the decision upon such motion shall be excluded in computing the time allowed for appeal.

Rule 80.—No officer shall entertain a motion in a case after an appeal from his decision has been taken.

3.—Appeals from the Commissioner to the Secretary.

Rule 81.—An appeal may be taken from the decision of the commissioner of the general land office to the Secretary of the interior upon any question relating to the disposal of the public lands and to private land claims, except in case of interlocutory orders and decisions and orders for hearing or other matter resting in the discretion of the commissioner. Decisions and orders forming the above exception will be noted in the record, and will be considered by the secretary on review in case an appeal upon the merits be finally allowed.

Rule 82.—When the commissioner considers an appeal defective, he will notify the party of the defect, and if not amended within fifteen days from the date of the service of such notice the appeal may be dismissed by the Secretary of the Interior and the case closed.

Rule 83.—In proceedings before the commissioner, in which he shall formally decide that a party has no right of appeal to the secretary, the party against whom such decision is rendered may apply to the secretary for an order directing the commissioner to certify said proceedings to the secretary, and to suspend further action until the secretary shall pass upon the same.

Rule 84.—Applications to the secretary under the preceding rule shall be made in writing, under oath, and shall fully and specifically set forth the grounds upon which the application is made.

Rule 85.—When the commissioner shall formally decide against the right of an appeal, he shall suspend action on the case at issue for twenty days from service of notice of his decision, to enable the party against whom the decision is rendered to apply to the secretary for an order, in accordance with Rules 83 and 84.

Rule 86.—Notice of appeal from the commissioner's decision must be filed in the general land office and served on the appellee or his counsel within sixty days from the date of the service of notice of such decision.

Rule 87.—When notice of the decision is given through the mails by the register and receiver, or surveyor-general, five days additional will be allowed by those officers for the transmission of the letter and five days for the return of the appeal through the same channel before reporting to the general land office.

Rule 88.—Within the time allowed for giving notice of appeal the appellant shall also file in the general land office a specification of errors, which specification shall clearly and concisely designate the error of which he complairs.

Rule 89.—He may also, within the same time, file a written argument, with citation of authorities, in support of his appeal.

Rule 90.—A failure to file specification of errors within the time required will be treated as a waiver of the right of appeal, and the case will be considered closed.

Rule 91.—The appellee will be allowed thirty days from the expiration of the sixty days allowed for appeal in which to file his argument.

Rule 92.—The appellant shall be allowed thirty days from service of argument of appellee in which to file argument strictly in reply, and no other or further arguments or motions of any kind shall be filed without permission of the commissioner or secretary and notice to the opposite party.

Rule 93.—A copy of the notice of appeal, specification of errors, and all arguments of either party, shall be served on the opposite party within the time allowed for filing the same.

Rule 94.—Such service shall be made personally or by registered letter.

Rule 95.—Proof of personal service shall be the written acknowledgement of the party served, or the affidavit of the person making the service attached to the papers served, and stating time, place and manner of service.

Rule 96.—Proof of service by registered letter shall be the affidavit of the person mailing the letter attached to a copy of the postoffice receipt.

Rule 97.—Fifteen days, exclusive of the day of mailing, will be allowed for the transmission of notices and papers by mail, except in case of notice to resident attorneys, when one day will be allowed.

Rule 98.—Notice of interlocutory motions and proceedings before the commissioner and secretary shall be served personally or by registered letter, and service proved as provided in Rules 94 and 95.

Rule 99.—No motion affecting the merits of the case or the regular order of proceedings will be entertained except on due proof of service notice.

Rule 100.—*Ex parte* cases, and cases in which the adverse party does not appear, will be governed by the foregoing rules as to notices of decisions, time for appeal, and filing of exceptions and arguments, as far as applicable. In such cases, however, the right to file additional evidence at any stage of the proceedings to cure defects in the proof or record, will be allowed.

Rule 101.—No person hereafter appearing as a party or attorney in any case shall be entitled to a notice of the proceedings who does not at the time of his appearance file in the office in which the case is pending a statement in writing, giving his name and postoffice address and the name of the party whom he represents; nor shall any person who has heretofore appeared in a case be entitled to a notice unless within fifteen days after being requested to file such statement he shall comply with said requirements.

Rule 102.—No person not a party to the record shall intervene in a case without first disclosing, on oath, the nature of his interest.

Rule 103.—When the commissioner makes an order or decision affecting the merits of a case, or the regular order of proceedings therein, he will cause notice to be given to each party in interest whose address is known.

4.—Attorneys.

Rule 104.—In all cases, contested or *ex parte*, where the parties in interest are represented by attorneys, such attorneys will be recognized as fully controlling the cases of their respective clients.

Rule 105.—All notices will be served upon the attorneys of record.

Rule 106.—Notice to one attorney in a case shall constitute notice to all counsel appearing for the party represented by him, and notice to the attorney will be deemed notice to the party in interest.

Rule 107.—All attorneys practicing before the general land office and department of the Interior must first file the oath of office prescribed by section 3478, United States Revised Statutes.

Rule 108.—In the examination of any case, whether contested or *ex parte*, and for the preparation of arguments, the attorneys employed, when in good standing in the department, will be allowed full opportunity to consult the record of the case and to examine the abstracts, plats, field notes, and tract-books, and the correspondence of the general land office, or of the department relative thereto, and to make verbal inquiries of the various chiefs of divisions at their respective desks in respect to the papers or status of said case; but such personal inquiries will be made of no other clerk in the division except in the presence or with the consent of the head thereof, and will be restricted to the hours between 11 a. m. and 2 p. m.

Rule 109.—Any attorney detected in any abuse of the above privileges, or of gross misconduct, upon satisfactory proof thereof, after due notice and hearing, shall be prohibited from further practicing before the department.

Rule 110.—Should either party desire to discuss a case orally before the secretary opportunity will be afforded, at the discretion of the department, but only at a time specified by the secretary or fixed by stipulation of the parties, with the consent of the secretary, and in the absence of such stipulation or written notice to opposing counsel, with like consent, specifying the time when argument will be heard.

Rule 111.—The examination of cases on appeal to the commissioner or secretary will be facilitated by filing, in printed form, such arguments as it is desired to have considered.

5.—*Decisions.*

Rule 112.—Decisions of the commissioner not appealed from within the period prescribed become final, and the case will be regularly closed.

Rule 113.—The decision of the secretary, so far as respects the action of the executive, is final.

Rule 114.—Motions for review before the Secretary of the Interior and applications under Rules 83 and 84 shall be filed with the commissioner of the land office, who will thereupon suspend action under the decision sought to be reviewed and forward to the secretary such motion or application.

None of the foregoing rules shall be construed to deprive the Secretary of the Interior of the exercise of the directory and supervisory powers conferred upon him by law.

L. Q. C. LAMAR,
Secretary.

AMENDMENTS.

Rule 70 of Rules of Practice, approved Aug. 13, 1885, amended October 26, 1885, to read as follows:

"Rule 70.—Rules 43 and 49, inclusive, and rule 93 are not applicable to appeals from decisions rejecting applications to enter public lands."

Rule 81 of Rules of Practice, approved Aug. 13, 1885, amended December 8, 1885, so as to read as follows:

"No appeal shall be had from the action of the commissioner of the general land office affirming the decision of the local officers in any case where the party, or parties, adversely affected thereby shall have failed, after due notice, to appeal from such decision of said local officers.

"Subject to this provision an appeal may be taken from the decision of the commissioner of the general land office to the Secretary of the Interior upon any question relating to the disposal of the public lands and to private land claims, except in case of interlocutory orders and decisions and orders for hearing, and other matters resting in the discretion of the commissioner. Decisions and orders forming the above exception will be noted in the record, and will be considered by the secretary on review in case an appeal upon the merits be finally allowed."

Rule 108 of Rules of Practice, approved Aug. 13, 1885, amended January 11, 1886, so as to read as follows:

"In the examination of any case, whether contested or *ex parte*, the attorneys employed in said case, when in good standing before the department, for the preparation of arguments, will be allowed full opportunity to consult the records of the case, the abstracts, field notes, and tract-books, and the correspondence of the general land office or of the department not deemed *privileged* and *confidential;* and whenever, in the judgment of the commissioner, it would not jeopardize any public or official interest, may make verbal inquiries of chiefs of divisons at their respective desks in respect to the papers or status of said case; but such inquiries will not be made to said chiefs or other clerks of division except upon consent of the commissioner, assistant commissioner, or chief clerk, and will be restricted to hours between 11 a. m. and 2 p. m."

Rule 114 of Practice amended March 27, 1886, to read as follows:

"Motions for a review of decisions of the secretary should be filed with the secretary, who may, in his discretion, suspend action on the decision sought to be reviewed until such motion shall be considered."

The following amendment, approved March 27, 1886, to Rule 114 of Practice, to-wit:

Motions for a review of decisions of the secretary should be filed with the secretary, who may, in his discretion, suspend action on the decision sought to be reviewed until such motion shall be decided, is hereby revoked; and Rule 114 of Rules of Practice, approved Aug. 13, 1885, to-wit:

Motions for review before the Secretary of the Interior, and applications under Rules 83 and 84, shall be filed with the commissioner of the general land office, who will thereupon suspend action under the decision sought to be reviewed, and forward to the secretary such motion or application, will from this date (June 14, 1888) be in force.

S. M. STOCKSLAGER,
Commissioner.